HUMAN WORLDVIEW

Mohammad Ali Taheri

Published in the United States by Interuniversal Press.

First published in Farsi (Persian) in 2010

ISBN-10: 1939507111
ISBN-13: 978-1939507112
LCCN: 2013939698

Interuniversal Press

Table of Contents

Introduction

The human being, the most complex created being, has an existence as vast and magnificent as the entire universe. In case of negligence in acquiring the awareness and wisdom of himself and the universe, and not perceiving its greatness, he loses not only the ability for growth and transcendence but also the status of the superior creature. Therefore, he will not attain divine closeness and will always live in trouble and illness.

Most human problems are directly related to his point of view about the universe. Whenever his worldview is contrary to the truth and he judges external events and occurrences without awareness of natural laws, he is headed towards inner and external conflicts. Hence, not only will he lose his faith and feel perplexed and exposed in the universe, he will also suffer various types of illnesses due to the resultant emotional tensions. Consequently, living his life struggling with these complications, he will not benefit from his precious lifetime or fulfil his duty.

Based on this truth, one of the most indispensable duties of human beings is to discover the truths of the universe and restore its regulations. In this book you will find some of the most important principles and regulations that the author has acknowledged, so that you may study, contemplate and research it.

Chapter 1

The Role of Worldview in Life

Human beings have different reactions to each of the events and occurrences around them. The interesting point is that everyone's behavior and thoughts are also different, and each person has his own unique reaction to the same events; some of which can have a significant role in developing various diseases.

As will be discussed, one cause of human diseases is the person's reactions that result from his "worldview." Worldview mistakes (incorrect mental worldviews) develop diseases called **world-viewing diseases [mentosomatic or mind-body diseases]** in the individual.[1] For example, people have often suffered heart attacks, tremors, and other disorders the moment they hear the news about the sudden reduction of gold or foreign exchange price, and so on. This has been widely heard of around the world.

Due to certainty of these experiences in many people, questions arise: What is the relationship between the prices of gold, foreign exchange and the like, and the heart function? Why does it cause heart attack in some people and has no negative effects on the others? Or why do some people become ill when they hear of the death of their relatives and friends? Considering that medical science has found no clear

---

1- According to Halqeh mysticism, disorders are classified into: physical, psycheal, psychosomatic, mental, mentosomatic, mind-body-psyche and other disorders. For details please refer to the book Faradarmani by the same author.

relationship between events and the function of different parts of the human body, so why indeed does hearing a bad news cause positive or negative changes in our body, mind, and psyche (emotions)?

To answer these questions we first classify the causes of diseases in human beings. People become ill because of the different following reasons:

- Microorganisms contamination
- Old age, senility and fatigue
- Accidents
- Environmental pollution and poisons
- Malnutrition
- Absence of body movement
- **Incorrect worldview** (mentosomatic or mind-body diseases)
- Two-faced behaviors[2] (psychosomatic diseases)
- Congenital diseases and defects
- Others

In above categorization, *incorrect worldview* is one of the causes of human diseases. **Worldview** means the individual's general understanding of the environment and all the events occurring around him. In other

---

2- While interacting with the outside world events, an individual must often exhibit two-faced behaviors to better adapt to his environment (Two-faced behaviors compose a major part of our behaviors). As this behavior is not favourable or desirable for him, it can consequently lead to agitation, frustration, bottled up feelings, and so on, followed by the accumulation of a type of negative energy called the negative potential energy. When the quantity of such negative energy reaches a certain level, the individual will be taken to the High Court and goes through a one-way conviction. The reached [guilty] verdict is executed on the individual as a physical illness, which sometimes has no specific physical symptoms, yet one feels the pain and the related disabilities. As this type comes with no physical symptoms, the medical doctor would tell these patients that their problems are stress related, or more specifically, that they have psychosomatic illnesses. (For details please refer to the book Human From Another Outlook, by the same author).

words, everything that the human being comprehends from life events passes through the framework of the world-viewing software that is the extracted result of the *mind* [mental] and the *psyche*'s [psycheal] processing. This framework that automatically defines the individual's reactions to events is a [preliminary] software program and a filter located at the semi-conscious level. It is programmed consciously and is related to the individual's thinking based on his analytical method; however, its function is revealed unconsciously and automatically. It can therefore be considered as a semi-conscious program. As the above explanation shows, in comparison with the other unconscious human programs, the advantage of the *worldview* software is that its program can be consciously changed and advanced towards the desired direction.

All our emotions and feelings are defined in the **Psyche** [psycheal body][3], and all our perceptions, thoughts, understandings, and points of view about life are defined in the **Mind** [mental body][4].

The human mind has three sections: *conscious, semi-conscious* and *unconscious*. The operation of the conscious section is related to thought and decision-making. It spends time because it takes time for the *mind* to process and function consciously and make a decision accordingly.

The unconscious section presents people the results of predefined

---

3- Psyche or the psycheal body is one important body of man's existence that detects, examines, and displays the emotions, bringing about a sense of grief, rapture, fear, resentment, repulsion, happiness, misery, pride, hope, disappointment, disgrace, and so on. (For details please refer to Psyche, Human From Another Outlook, M.A. Taheri) .The psyche is divided into two sections: "Instinctive Psyche" and "Emotional Psyche".

4- Mental Body or Mind is one of the important human bodies. It is a management that organizes different sections and generally consists of the below subdivisions: • Memory and Archive of the Eternal Data • Memory Management • Data-Arranging Management (Creating Thoughts) • Cell and Body Management • Cell and Body Organization • Human Perception Organization • Data Organization (the eternal data archives). For details please refer to Mental body, Human From Another Outlook, M.A. Taheri

programs without spending time. The reactions of this section do not occur based upon the individual's thoughts and decision-making. Since this part has been programmed mainly in childhood and up to the age of five or six, changing its program in adulthood is extraordinarily difficult.[5]

However, the semi-conscious section operates according to predefined programs (institutionalized lifetime data). Its related actions and reactions are performed instantly and inadvertently and without decision-making (automatically). Different from the unconscious section, the semi-conscious section is accessible and changeable in adulthood and it can be reprogrammed if the individual decides to consciously change it or if they are convinced of its change.

Human worldview which was formed by childhood institutionalized data and subsequently affected and changed by adulthood accepted data, functions semi-consciously. The reactions of the *psyche* and the conscious section of the *mind* also play a role in changing the program.

The incidents and events around us are received by the brain's external

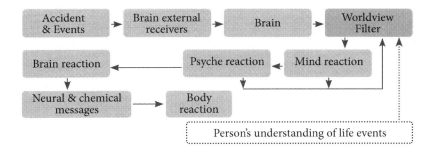

receivers or the five senses. Then they pass through the world-viewing framework and are evaluated. Worldview defines their weakness or strength, good or bad, beauty or unpleasantness, based on which an

---

5- One of the factors modifying this software is illumination and achieving inner perceptions.

individual feels prosperity or misery, lucky or unlucky.

Actually, after passing through this framework, the *mind*'s reaction to different events is revealed, and the individual's perception and understanding of the external events is determined. For example, each individual's perception and understanding of subjects such as death, birth, explosion, war, poverty, illness, and so on is dependent on this framework, and it is obvious that everybody has a different perception of such events.

After passing through the *mind* framework and producing mental perception and interpretations, it is the *psyche*'s turn to reveal the psycheal reaction to these events and phenomena. In this stage, the emotional reactions will be manifested (the events change to their emotional equivalent), and the feeling of happiness or sadness, aversion, hopelessness, vanity, and the like will appear.

In the next stage, the brain reacts in proportion to the mental-psycheal conclusions through creating chemical messages. These mental-psycheal moods are translated to the physical language. Finally, the body's reaction will follow.

For instance, suppose that some people are sitting in a room and they suddenly hear a loud explosion from outside. Each of the individuals' brain auditory receivers (ears) receives the explosion sound and everybody becomes aware of the explosion. However, each individual shows a different reaction and the level of fear or horror of each person varies. The reason for this difference is that the data of all events are passed through the individual's personal world-viewing framework and filter which is called "**the Worldview Filter**". This filter has been programmed beforehand to analyze and interpret events, and the weakness or strength, and pleasantness or unpleasantness of events is determined based on it. It is after this stage that the *mind*'s perceptual reaction to that incident is evaluated and our perception regarding the phenomena is determined (for instance, in this stage it will be evaluated whether this explosion is dangerous). Then the *psyche* manifests our emotions to that event (for instance, the *psyche* determines whether the event is pleasing or not). In fact, the *psyche*'s emotional reaction reveals our emotional and sentimental evaluations.

Following the evaluation of the *mind* and *psyche*, the brain's reaction begins and the translation of emotional states into the physical language of the body appears as chemical reactions. It is after this translation that the physical effects such as pale skin, hand or body tremor, cheek blushing, and the like appear on the body. For each person, these states are specified and evaluated according to their strength/weakness, pleasantness/unpleasantness and so on. In general, the meaning that each event carries or the perceptual and emotional load it transfers is defined when passing through this filter.

In the above explosion event, all the people do not feel the same level of fear and so they will experience different reactions. In other words, the same incident elicits different reactions because the strength or weakness of the event will be uniquely specified by each individual's world-viewing filter.

Now an important question arises. For instance, does the brain first confront fear and then order secretion of adrenalin, or has adrenalin been first secreted by the brain and after that the person is filled with fear?

Based on the evaluation of the worldview filter which defines the level of fear, the brain is ordered to send out the required reaction. Subsequently, the brain orders the relevant section to secrete chemical messages. In fact, the factor that determines the type and number of chemical messages during different events is the *worldview filter*.

As mentioned, a person first encounters events, evaluates them, and then the chemical reactions are ordered to be produced. Therefore, the section responsible for the evaluation of life events and incidents has the most important role, and we have to program it so that events have minimal impact on us and will not pose a health risk. Here, the brain is only a connector with the role of translating our perceptions and our emotions into the language of the physical body.

In medical cures, the transmission of chemical messages via hormones [and neurotransmitters] is only considered. For instance, if the secretion balance of each chemical compound is disturbed, drugs will be used to restore its equilibrium. However, if before the primary orders are sent to the brain, we program the correct orders in the world-viewing filter, events will no longer be able to change the brain's chemical balance.

Now, in the above example, suppose that another explosion happens one hour after the first one. In this case our reaction might not be the same as the former one. Since it is the worldview filter that determines the quality, formation and type of the messages, in case of repetition, we may have a weaker or stronger reaction.

Consider another example: if a person wears a frightening mask and suddenly appears in front of a group of people, there will be as many reactions as there are people. One individual might have no reaction while another might faint. Nevertheless, in case of repetition, the sharper reactions become smoother and if continued the fear might vanish.

Sometimes people are depressed by events but will others also be depressed by the same events? Of course, the answer is negative. Everybody sees occurrences and world events through the spectacles of their own worldview, and they see the universe in the color that their worldview spectacles define. Therefore, each person interprets and explains life and the universe according to his spectacles, and the event which depresses someone might not have the same effect for others.

For this reason, the worldview filter should be studied anew due to its determining role in many diseases. By correcting our worldview and becoming equipped with the correct ones we can prevent many diseases and overcome many problems. On the contrary, if an accurate description is not presented for the world-viewing filter and if no attempt is made for its correction, we will be exposed to numerous problems and diseases.

The *world-viewing filter* is software and our point of view and instant decisions depend on its programs. Therefore, the method of programming this software is important because it could be programmed correctly or incorrectly. If we succeed to write the correct programs we can have the best decisions and reactions in our lives. For instance, one person experiences problems and becomes ill when faced with financial issues, but others never experience any psycheal, mental, or somatic problems from the same trigger. Our individual reactions in facing events relate to our filter programming.

As a matter of fact, except for poisons, micro-organisms, accidents, events, environmental pollution, etc that harm human health, incorrect worldviews in analysing external events can also seriously jeopardize one's health and bring about physical disorders. Because worldview reveals our mental evaluations of all the events around us and the universe, which is then followed by the reactions of the *psyche* and the body. Thus, if the *mind* is not programmed correctly, it can cause *mentosomatic* or *mind-body* diseases.

One of the characteristics of mentosomatic diseases is that they appear suddenly and abruptly while **psychosomatic (Psyche-body)**[6] diseases appear eventually and over a long time.

6- Please refer to footnote number 2.

Human worldview has a mutual relationship with the other parts of the *mind*, and worldview problems and their negative effect on the *mind* can cause physical disorders. For instance, incorrect worldview can indirectly cause *lack of integrity (unity) of the mind* which is one of the factors of contracting mentosomatic diseases.

The *mind* is one of the management sections of human beings, and its subsections, each with their own detailed subsets, include the following:

• Management and organizing the body and cells

• Management and organizing human perceptions

• Management and organizing data (archive of information)

A disturbed and deranged mind cannot manage the human body perfectly. Thus, a person with such a disturbed mind will be highly vulnerable to diseases that are a result of disturbed cells and body program. Different types of cancers are examples of such disturbances wherein the cells lose their program and are divided constantly, or in other cases the cells' normal functionality decrease and organ atrophy happens.

Preventing mind disturbance has been one of humankind's greatest efforts across time as he soon discovered that this inner factor is controlling and disabling his thought and is taking him wherever it wants. For several thousands of years human beings have wanted to control and achieve dominance over their thoughts but this inner factor that disturbs the mind's integrity is preventing them from doing so. It is anti-Kamal[7] (acts against the Kamal pathway) since the disturbed mind cannot think properly about the universe and its whyness. This

---

7- The term Kamal literally means completeness, and refers to the human's spiritual growth towards completion (perfection). It includes self-realization and self-awareness, meaning clarity of vision about the universe, from where and for what purpose we have come, and where we are heading to. The human being is constantly dealing with two forces and attractions; one is towards spirituality and Kamal-seeking, and the other is the anti-Kamal or Kamal-thwarting force.

bothering factor constantly drifts the individual around until he finally becomes tired from such mental detours and without achieving any positive results, stops trying.

In general, a person has two groups of selves within himself who are in conflict. Each group of the *selves* wants to draw the individual towards a direction; one group towards Kamal and the other towards anti-Kamal.

One of these anti-Kamal *selves* is the one that does not allow the individual's *mind* to remain present at one moment and place, and to be wherein the person [actually] is. This preventing factor plays with time, place, and the like [*mind* disturbance]. For instance, if we are in the present time it will take us to the past or future, or else, it takes our *mind* from where we are to other places[8], and sometimes engages it with various subjects that are not related to the individual's present time.

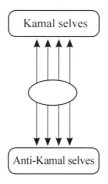

The area of conflict between the two selves

8- For instance, when you are at work, it takes you to your house and makes you think to yourself that if you were home right now, you would be doing a different thing, and when you are at home, it takes you to other places such as work.

A person with a disturbed *mind* also continues the same processing of the day during sleep. During sleep the *mind* has the duty of sorting out the day's data files and placing them correctly, so that they are easily accessible when required and the person can have a competent memory. Additionally, it removes the stresses and tensions of the data (created during the day) in order that no tension remains in the body after sleeping.

The main duty of the [*mind's*] body and cell management and organization is specifying the duty description of bodily constituents through *consciousness distribution*. If the manager does not present a correct order and duty description for the cells, they will [either] face abnormal growth (cancers) or decrease in normal function (organ disability). This is because a large part of the body's management energies are dissipated due to incorrect worldview. Some of the problems resulting in dissipation of *mind* energy are as follows;

- Excessive engagement of the *mind* with subjects that have simply nothing to do with the individual and have no important role in his life

- Discrimination and multiplicity due to incorrect worldview

- Pointless judgments caused by incorrect worldview

Discrimination and Multiplicity-seeking

The *mind's* struggle with the unity of the universe[9] and fragmenting it through bias means multiplicity-viewing and discriminating among the universe's constituents and it wastes a great deal of the *mind's* energy. There is a verse from Sohrab Sepehri[10] that explains this subject

---

9- The universe is integral and all of its constituents are related to each other as a Unified Body; as unified elements of one body or whole.
10- Sohrab Sepehri (1928 - 1980) was a notable modern Persian poet and one of Iran's foremost modernist painters.

beautifully:

> *I don't know why they say that the horse is a gentle animal or the*
> *pigeon is beautiful!*
> *And why nobody has a vulture in the cage!*
> *What does clover have less than the red tulip?!*
> *Eyes should be washed*
> *Looking should be made in another way!*
> *The words should be washed*
> *Words themselves should be the wind, should be the rain.*

Pointless Judgments Caused by Incorrect Worldviews

When a pedestrian who is walking through the street evaluates every single aspect of other people's appearance such as their fatness, thickness, beauty and ugliness, tallness and shortness, and every now and then even judges their inner characteristics (such as good- or bad-hearted, etc.), the individual consumes and wastes an extremely great deal of mental energy; hence, the *mind*'s management is disturbed and becomes tired. As a result, the management and handling of the individual's body is disrupted.

In general, since the human beings *mind* energy is limited, a program is required for using this energy which is to be studied under the title of **mental energy management**.

Chapter 2

Worldview Problems

The most important worldview principles that rule human life are as follows. Not being equipped with these principles can cause problems and result in diseases:

1. knowledge, understanding, and perception of the universe and its regulations and principles

2. Knowledge, understanding, and perception of the Dipolar world [world of dual contrasts]

3. Knowledge, understanding, and perception of journey and destination

4. Knowledge, understanding, and perception of the end and the means

5. Knowledge, understanding, and perception of Worldly Love

6. Knowledge, understanding, and perception of peace [with God, the universe, one's self and others]

7. Knowledge, understanding, and perception of time (asymphasis with time)

8. Knowledge, understanding, and perception of the heaven (asymphasis with the heaven)

9. Knowledge, understanding, and perception of integration and unity of the *mind*.

10. Knowledge, understanding, and perception of emotional maturity.

11. ...

1. Absence of knowledge, understanding, and perception of the universe and its regulations and principles

Absence of knowledge, understanding and perception of the material world is one of the main and deeply rooted problems in human worldview. The universe is similar to a book that teaches human beings the regulations of life, and not paying attention to this book results in the individuals' discordance with the universe, as well as making serious irreparable mistakes in life. It is through this book, which contains God's apparent signs that have been exposed to each and every human being throughout history and all around the world, that He presents humankind the principles of viewing life and dealing with it in order to program their 'worldview'.

> *For whoever perceives himself as a divine manifestation*
> *The entire world is a divine book*
> *- Sheik Mahmood Shabestari*

As a matter of fact, the material world is a [symbolic] illuminating book of His divine and apparent signs, and it is by reading this book that one can discover the basis of a correct way of thinking and program the right worldview.

> *Indeed, in the creation of the skies and the earth, in the passage of*
> *day and night, there are signs for the wise.*
> *-Quran; Sura 3, Verse 190*

Human beings require guides to move them towards Kamal and transcendence, called *'guidance mediators'*. Thus, all the elements such as different objects, plants, animals and human beings that help individuals to understand and perceive the laws governing the universe in any [possible] form are in this category.

The nightingale noted a sweet singing over the cypress tree
It was the spiritual mediators' lesson last night
It meant come and see how the fire of Moses transformed into a
flower
And listen to the monotheism that the tree speaks of

-Hafez

For man to move on God's path and towards Him, he must essentially use all equipment and facilities:

And seek equipment and facilities towards Him.

-Quran; Sura Maedeh, Verse 35

The universal book is one of such equipment, and each and every particle of it holds lessons for human being to achieve Kamal.

"I remember that many years ago when I felt deeply depressed and hopeless, I went to the mountains. I was aimlessly climbing when I came across a large rock. I began to observe it carefully and suddenly noticed a very strange phenomenon; a plant was sprouting from inside the rock. Seeing this scene all of a sudden brought this message that: even from the heart of a rough rock, one can bud."

All the holy books invite people to deeply think and contemplate the book of the universe. The greatest sin might be that an individual dies without understanding the laws and principles governing the universe. By comprehending these laws, the foundation of the individual's worldviews is drawn from the illuminating book of His divine and apparent signs. The absence of this understanding is one of the main factors that cause worldview problems and mentosomatic diseases.

Several laws of the universe include [but are not limited to] the following:

- Relativity Law

- Perihelion and Aphelion Law (Fountain Law)
- Order & Disorder Law
- Weed Law
- Dipolar World Law
- Action & Reaction Law
- Conflict Law
- Uniqueness & Non-Repeatability Law
- Dynamic in Static Law
- Birth & Death Law
- Law of Change

2. Absence of Knowledge, Understanding, and Perception of the Dipolar World

One of human's major worldview problems is the absence of knowledge, understanding and perception of the Dipolar world. This means that humankind has not discovered the essence and purpose of the **Dipolar world (world of dual opposites or contrasts)**, and even those who are aware, disregard it in practice.

The basis of the Dipolar world wherein human being has been placed is two poles (opposites) or conflicts. God created the two positive and negative networks and placed human beings in a position to choose between the two networks. He placed the dual tendencies towards the two opposite networks inside humans so that they willingly select one and move towards it:

> *Then, virtuousness or virtue-less-ness was inspirited to him (human being).*
>
> -Quran; Sura Shams, Verse 8.

This is a key test to develop experience and maturity; otherwise, no transcendent experience would ever have been brought to the universe. But human beings forget where they are and why this world has been created so full of conflicts. A world that runs with corruption, oppression, injustice and the like on one side, and truth, justice, sacrifice, devotion and the like on the other. Some people think that there has been a mistake in the plan of Creation and that God is unaware or indifferent to human's oppression and corruption on Earth. Whereas, due to the angels dominance on the dimension of time (and the lack of time)[1], from the very beginning of creation even the angels knew about future events and human behavior.

Almost all people -when faced with oppression and injustice-instantly complain to God about why oppression and injustice exists. They sometimes cry angrily, 'Where is God?' when they find oppression, injustice, poverty, starvation and the like. They say, 'Don't You see how the world is suffering oppression and injustice?' After this complaint some say, 'I don't believe in this God anymore.'

They forget that the designer and creator of good and evil is God Himself, and that if He did not want evil on Earth, He would have created a world without any oppression and corruption. If so, this world would have been only for angels and the art of human beings in overcoming evil would have never been manifested in the universe.

If we question -as an objection- why the pharaoh and others like him were even created, or ask why oppression exists, then we are ignoring one important matter; the creation of dual opposites or the Dipolar world. And that we stand in the middle of its two opposite poles to experience the divine against the evil through a great test; and to ultimately find the path towards Kamal with our own choice and move

---

1- This refers to the Unipolar world which is a world that can be described, but has no conflict and lacks the dimensions of space and time (Halqeh mysticism, M.A. Taheri).

from darkness towards light, and hence reveal our special capability in the universe. However, if there were no opposites and no selection and if we were in a Unipolar world (with only one pole), we would have escaped this test. In that case the question would not exist and the plan of human's creation would not lead to any purpose.

In fact, oppression and injustice and the like are the essentials and inseparable factors of the Dipolar world, and through achieving its awareness and perceptions, humankind must deter from them and never be willing to oppress others or the universe.[2] We can choose to stand up to oppression or accompany it. In other words, we can select Imam Hossein's[3] or Yazid's pathway.

Therefore, the law of opposites governs the material world, and the human being is placed at the heart of these dual opposites and is not apart from it. He must define his position within it and find his duty and fulfil it instead of objecting the law itself and asking why dipolarity exists. We have to consider these points and also know that not perceiving the dipolarity that governs human life and objecting its existence, itself intensifies the conflict between human beings and God. Besides not solving any problems it also creates more confusion and anxiety. In addition, bringing up such questions and objections wastes the individual's mental energy and causes nervousness, anxiety

---

2- Please refer to lack of knowledge, understanding, and perception of reconciliation (peace), peace with the universe, in the same chapter.

3- Invitations like Imam Hossein's call [the third Imam of Shia Muslims who was killed in the 61st lunar year by Yazid in Karbala desert (Iraq)] of 'Is there anyone to help me?', is one of the most recognized calls against fighting oppression in history, and those who have reached the necessary awareness have answered it. This invitation is bereft of the meaning and sense of extreme destitution, and creates the last opportunity for finding oneself and meditating, an opportunity for thinking about one's own Kamal and making a decision about eliminating oppression and creating justice, which is closely related to Kamal. (For details please refer to 'what is oppression', A Collection of Article, by the same author.)

and the like, and has no other results other than diseases.

Human being has not started his life on Earth to object to the creation of dipolarity. He has been created to gain control over its dual opposites and in so doing, exhibit his existential capabilities to the universe; the very capabilities of which God -with His knowledge- responded to the angels' objection to the creation of man:

I know something that you all do not know.
-Quran; Sura Baqare, Verse 30

3. Absence of Knowledge, Understanding, and Perception of Journey and Destination

Humans are constantly seeking destinations and designing paths to reach them. Here a question arises: Is only the destination important and not the journey itself?

Suppose that we are taking a trip with a certain destination. We have selected the best route and the best vehicle. In this case is it only important to reach the destination and is going through the journey of no value? In general, is the journey more important in life or the destination?

For further illustration of the question, let us imagine an example of this issue. Consider that you want to go to a trip by bus from Tehran to Zahedan[4]. In the beginning of the trip, one of the passengers stands up and says to the audience, 'Ladies and Gentlemen! I am a magician and I can do something extraordinary for you. I have the power to decrease the long trip to Zahedan to the twinkling of an eye. You will arrive at your destination right away and the long tiresome trip will only take a second. Do you want me to do this amazing job for you?'

What do you guess the passengers will decide to do? How many

4- Zahedan is a south eastern city of Iran and the capital of Sistan and Baluchestan province.

people would like the magician to carry out this astounding act and decrease the twenty hour bus drive into the twinkling of an eye? We can surmise that nearly all of them will agree with this proposal.

For further clarification let us consider another example. Suppose that the same magician asks newly pregnant ladies, 'Do you want me to pass the nine months period of pregnancy in the twinkling of an eye so you can give birth to your baby right away?' They might all want to deliver their babies at that very minute. Now suppose that all the babies have been born, and the magician again asks the mothers, 'Do you want to bring up your babies to one year old in the twinkling of an eye so they are now old enough to start to talk and say sweet words? Now do you want to watch your children at three years old when they can run and play? Do you desire to see your children even grow more and go to school? What about going to the university? Do you want to see them right now as they are getting married? [And all the subsequent phases of life's journey]'

In other cases such as obtaining educational credentials, driving licenses, and the like, how many people agree to obtain their required credentials straight away? What about purchasing a house, car, etc? How many people would love to have time collapsed to immediately obtain their desires?

We must acknowledge that nearly everyone is ready to skip time. They would like the magician to take them immediately to their desires and in exchange they are willing to give all the hours of the journey to the magician without delay.

Now, we return to the original question, 'Is going through the journey more valuable in life or arriving at the destination?' To answer this question we must realize that 'our lifetime is our capital.' This capital (lifetime) is equal to the sum of the journeys' durations and the destinations' arrival times.

> **Lifetime = journey duration + destination arrival time**

Passing through each journey takes a certain amount of time. For instance, the time required for travelling from Tehran to Zahedan is twenty hours by bus. However, arriving at each destination takes no more than a second. In our example it equals braking the car. At the instant that the bus arrives at the terminal and the driver stops the vehicle, we have arrived at the destination and the path has ended. Here, the passengers' desire for reaching this city has been attained. From this point, though, another destination starts, and all the passengers are looking for other paths to reach their next destination. Thus, they have to pass through another journey to reach the new destination. Life is a series of passing through such journeys and destinations.

The time of destination arrival is zero (an instant). For instance, despite several months of effort and the time spent, we get our driver's license in a second. This means that we consider the destination which is getting the driver's license and make our best efforts to finally get hold of the license, but the very second we get it (destination arrival time) the destination has ended. Another example: to purchase an apartment, we strive several years until one day in the notary public it is finally notarized 'sold', and we sign it. As soon as we remove our hand from the paper, this destination is also reached.

Therefore, the time of reaching the destination(s) is about zero seconds. So, a lifetime is actually equal to the time of travelling the path(s). As a matter of fact, life is the journey itself.

> **Life= the time of travelling on the path(s)**

However, in most people's lives, destinations are only important, and they do not wish for the paths that lead them to these destinations. They all sacrifice the journeys to their destinations because they are extremely eager to traverse the paths quickly and wish for time to pass fast so they can arrive at their desired destinations sooner. These destinations are sometimes places (a city,..) and sometimes goals like having a baby, obtaining educational certification, purchasing a house and the like.

Human beings are appointing destinations every second. As soon as they determine a destination, they become focused on it and will not notice the path. They are willing to speed through the entire time of the journey in a second and instead attain their appointed goal. Consequently, they do not benefit from the path as they ought to and do not enjoy it. This way they do not live fully.

After having spent years of their lives, everyone declares, 'I don't know why life passed in a flash'. They are usually unaware that they should blame themselves for not caring for the journey times and only thinking about the destinations. Therefore, a person who spends his lifetime barely thinking about destinations without paying attention to the life's journey has lost his entire life.

We often hear people saying 'I wish I could quickly pass these months until I got married' or 'I wish I could pass these ten years sooner to finish my house payments.' They are not aware that once their bank payments are finished, ten years of their lives has also passed. And that they have lost the most important capital, their lifetime. Accordingly, we should never have an exclusive look on our goals and desires, or hope for the time to come when our house payments and the like are over.

Human beings are faced with two kinds of invisible and dangerous termites:

(1) The termite of **'what would have happened if …?'**

(2) The termite of **'when …?'**

These two types of termites eat away human life. They do not let us live our lives and deprive the individuals of all their journeys. While on the journey, most people ask themselves all the time: 'When do we reach the destination?' This termite does not allow them to pay attention to the journey and enjoy it. Then, at the end of the path, they are fatigued due to experiencing the journey's heavy stress and agitation. As a result, their bodies are poisoned and they are entirely impatient and nervous.

Considering the way that human being's eyes are fixed on the ends and the way that they are rapidly ignoring the journeys, they will suddenly find themselves near the tomb where they meet the same magician who asks them, 'Do you want me to help you rush through the death ceremonies and bury you as soon as possible?' Maybe this time they shout with no voice and say, 'NO! I don't want this destination. I don't want any destination. And I wish I had never wanted any destinations.'

As we have seen, the human being is the killer of '*time*.' He is endlessly eliminating the paths towards his goals. In fact, he is losing the time that he kills. Therefore, one of the witnesses that testify against him is '*time*' (*I swear by the time, surely, the human is in a (state of) loss -Quran; Sura Al-Asr, Verse 1-2*). Human beings greatly oppress themselves with such a loss. It is indeed an irretrievable oppression because '*time*' is the most essential capital that individuals have to invest in their lives. And this capital constantly decreases while humans speed its reduction.

With regard to the effect that struggling for the journey has on the appearance of diseases, it should be pointed out that when the individual does not care for the path and wants time to pass more quickly to reach the destination, and considering that it is not promptly achievable as per the person's desire, s/he feels distressed, spasmodic, nervous, irritable and anxious. All of which lead to the secretion of chemical poisons in the body, ultimately causing illnesses.

Consequently, human beings must live through the path(s), enjoy them and never want the path to end. Otherwise, they seek death without benefiting from life. All of us must realize that after completing a journey and arriving at its destination, we take a step towards our tomb. And one day we will regret not comprehending the values of the life's journeys.

4. Absence of Knowledge, understanding, and Perception of the End and the Means

What is the end and what is the means? This is an important question that we all face in life. The importance of this question is that all equipment has an expiry date, and if we consider any equipment as the destination, our life foundation will be unstable and may crumble at any moment.

If we ask the elderly about their goal of living and what they have tried to achieve in life, the majority of them are likely to talk about bringing up their children, preparing educational opportunities for them, their marriage, and the like. In fact, many people only live for their children.

If we ask the same question from a professor at a university, they will mainly talk about their efforts for teaching and training hundreds of educated people such as doctors, engineers, etc, and how they have served the society and the world of science. In other words, the goal of a group of people is scientific services.

What is our own answer to this question?

Science, health, wealth, power, reputation, religion, children, spouse, peace, happiness, serving people, serving God, freedom, marriage, love, mysticism and the like are only the equipment for achieving one [single] goal that cannot be anything other than '*Kamal*'. For instance, education is [an equipment] to follow another goal. Religion is a means for guidance. And serving people is a means for [spiritual] elevation.

Therefore, there is only one worthwhile goal, and except it, everything else is nothing but equipment. All equipment is for our elevation and movement towards the destination of Kamal. Here, Kamal signifies the Absolute Kamal (God), and moving towards God is fulfilled by moving towards the self. The word '*God*' serves as a reminder that we as humans should become 'Aware of Ourselves'.

One of the major worldview problems that lead to diseases is the absence of knowledge of the end and the means (equipment). We can select either the end or the means as the pillar of our life. If one's pillar of life and entire lifetime investment is on equipment such as wealth, power, children, spouse and the like, the result will be nothing but loss and harm, because equipment may disappear in a moment and is impermanent. For instance, the child may be undutiful, the spouse may leave [or die], and the wealth may be dissipated. Even if we construct our life based on science, we should know that we are likely to lose our memory in an accident and even forget our own name.

However, if the goal and basis of our life is Kamal, it is everlasting and despite all that changes in our life, and whether or not the equipment are there or not, our destination (Kamal) is fixed. For this reason, our life should be based on the stable foundation and not on an inconstant and variable one.

The human being loves the *summit*. He naturally tends to elevation and Kamal-seeking. Most of us, without even being aware of this truth, unconsciously enjoy the summit. We sometimes find this summit in mountain climbing, in flying, or even in compiling wealth, [increasing] proficiency in work, and so on.

If we liken the movement towards Kamal to climbing a mountain and moving towards its peak, we can better observe some of the rules of such movement. Mountain climbing or conquering the peak has certain rules. For example, a professional climber, based on what he can afford, prepares the best climbing equipment. Lightness and competency is of importance to him and he is not stingy with it. On the path towards Kamal it is also essential to use the best and simplest facilities (equipment). Using difficult and complex words and idioms is not suitable for elevation and Kamal.

Unprofessional mountain climbers are divided into two groups. The first group prepares beautiful and famous brand equipment. During climbing they only pay attention to their equipment and style, and climb the mountain slope to a certain level but never focus on the top.

The second group carries very heavy equipment. On the mountain slope we see these people carrying a huge stereo system for listening to loud music, with a big watermelon in one arm and a barbeque on their back. Seeing them, you immediately guess that they do not have the slightest intention to climb the mountain. First, they change their path and instead of climbing the mountain, turn towards the valley and sit by the river. Then they prepare the barbecue to cook kebab, they put the watermelon in the cold river water, and disturb the quiet of the mountain with loud music. They look at the climbers and chuckle at them, and say, 'Why do they take all the trouble to go to the top of the mountain!'

The professional climber has obtained the best shoes; however, contrary to the first group, after wearing them he only focuses on the top of the mountain. He considers selecting and using the best equipment important, but as soon as he starts to climb, the price or the equipment is itself insignificant. A professional climber only concentrates on the peak and nothing distracts them.

The human being who moves on the pathway to Kamal can also prepare and use the best equipment (facilities) for living, but everywhere he goes, his *Axis of Existence*[5] should be the axis of Kamal. This way, even his best equipment loses their importance. The Kamal-seeking individual (climber) always gazes at the peak of his destination and not at the climbing equipment.

As discussed, a professional climber contrary to the second group prepares the most efficient and lightest equipment. In this regard, in the pathway of mysticism and Kamal, our '*Nazar*'[6] is only important, and there is absolutely no need for any techniques or [special] equipment, or carrying and wearing something [such as rings, symbols, verses ...]. These are nothing more than extra load that makes the trip longer.

5- If thinking about Kamal is institutionalized in human existence, not only are our thoughts directed towards Kamal, but also our Axis of Existence will be in line with Kamal. In more precise terms, if someone comes to the mystical understanding that wherever they look they see God, and when faced with something that is admirable and praiseworthy, they entirely pay attention to God and believe that all praise is due to God (they have achieved the truth of 'Praise be to God'), then their Axis of Existence, which is the most hidden dimension of each person, will correspond to Kamal. People's appearance, behavior, and speech cannot reveal compliance or incompliance of their Axis of Existence with Kamal (whether their Axis of Existence is positive or negative), and even they themselves may be unaware of that state of compliance/incompliance. But this Axis of Existence leaves traces in all the works of an individual as positive or negative emissions of consciousness. (For details please refer to Human Insight, by the same author)

6- Nazar is a 'brief attention' or 'glance' and is a fleeting moment of attention with the purpose of establishing a link or connection to the Interuniversal Consciousness. Here, we are dealing with an indescribable definition. 'Intension' is definable as an inner willing or similar terms, but Glance is even shorter than the intension; it is rather instantaneous, even a 'brief attention' is not an appropriate term here (Human From Another Outlook, M.A. Taheri).

Kamal is not attained by carrying or wearing anything. Mysticism (*Erfan*) is an inner transformation and does not have any external (observable) display. It ends up in '*Nazar*'.

Another point is that professional climbers never climb the arduous high mountain paths alone. They consider it an important principle to never go climbing without an accompanier, because the path is extremely dangerous without them and their cooperation. Therefore, if an individual decides to climb the mountain alone and even should he come down healthily, the other professional climbers will reprimand him. Similarly, in the path towards Kamal we should not climb alone, because the presence of the accompaniers decreases the risk of mistakes and falling down. And in case of an error one can benefit from their assistance.

Even if a person, who only cares about his own climbing, does attain Kamal, he will be asked: Why did you think only about yourself and come alone? Desiring Kamal only for oneself is a sign of selfishness and egocentricity and is considered anti-Kamal. It resembles an individual who only rescues himself from a fire accident, and despite having the chance, s/he does nothing for the others. In *Erfan* (mysticism), salvation is collective (group) and not individual.[7]

The reasons for *Erfan*'s collective nature are:

1- In mysticism selfishness and egocentricity are put aside.

> *Until you think about yourself, you won't be forgiven*
> *Until you are selfish, nothing will be shown to you*
> *Until you are not free from yourself and the two worlds,*
> *Do not knock on the door, because it will not be opened to you*
> *-Sheik Mahmood Shabestari*

7- For details please refer to the book Human and Insight, collective movement, M.A. Taheri.

2- In the Kamal pathway, attending to people is the same as attending to God.

The rank of '*effaced*' and '*fanaa*'[8] is valuable when the individual has attained it by living beside other people and associating and sympathizing with them. As the next stage, all those who attain the rank of '*God-Faded*' return among other people to invite them to the path. This stage is called '*People-Faded*'.

Making peace with God and communicating with Him is easier than making peace with the people. In truth, we cannot attain Kamal only by making peace with God and without making peace with the people. Therefore, in Kamal's framework, reaching harmony and peace with the others is considered a valuable art and is one of the primary principles.

3- To promote Kamal, the level of the society's Kamal should necessarily be improved.

The human beings can be compared to the birds flying together within a net. Despite a bird's eagerness to ascend to the heights, the level of flight is always determined by the birds flying at the lowest level. Hence, in order to ascend, they should all move together. Similarly, human beings' lives are not independent of one another. And to ascend the Kamal pathway it is necessary for us to be accompanied by one another.

One of the principles of mountain climbing is that a mountaineer ought to stop at stations on the path to rest and refresh. These stations may have beautiful sightseeing. In such case the mountaineer should

---

8- Fanaa is a state in which an individual is lost in the divine majesty and eliminates self. The greater such loss, the less the individual sees themselves, until they no longer see themselves and achieve the status of 'faqr'. Eliminating 'the self' in mystical exploration and transformation is a type of transcendental nonexistence because it makes God manifest for the mystic; therefore, it is highly important. (Human and Insight, the collective Ettesal, M.A. Taheri)

not become so attracted to these views that he forgets climbing to the top. He must not let the destination be affected by the beauty of the views. Thus, after enjoying the beautiful landscape, he must essentially leave the station and once more continue his main path to the top. Otherwise, the marginal beauties can totally prevent us from achieving our destination.

This is an important point in the Kamal path, and so we must pay attention to this mystical advice: 'When you arrive at a garden, pick a flower and keep going'. It might seem that the pleasure-seeking people advise this, but this phrase is anyhow very instructive for mystics and Kamal-seekers.

Finding the best path to climb to the top is another important principle in mountain climbing. For this purpose, one should either seek the assistance of a guide or have the accurate map at hand to be able to easily pass the barriers and arduous ways and safely reach the destination without deviation from the path.

The risk of deviation and falling down also exists when climbing the path to the Kamal peak. Hence, in order to differentiate between going along the path and going astray, the individual must be aware of the path's principles and benefit from aware guides who know the way. Throughout history there have been many cases of people on the spiritual path who intended to climb to the top; however, without knowing, they went astray. Not only did they deprive themselves of Kamal, instead, they became ignorant worshipers of God who acted against the truth in the name of the truth!

Therefore, the following climbing principles can promise the enthusiastic Kamal climbers a successful attainment of the summit:

1- Moving together [collective (group) movement]

2- Using light and at the same time the highest quality equipment

3- Avoiding carrying unnecessary equipment

4- Avoiding stopping permanently for beautiful sightseeing during the climb

5- Recognizing the right path

As previously mentioned, one of the worldview problems is that some individuals spend too much of their lifetime and mental energy on children, spouse, or on other people. In a sense, they become the individual's actual goal in life. However, in the journey to Kamal's peak all people are considered companions and they can only assist us in moving ahead. Furthermore, since the place of spouse, children, and others are studied within this framework, they are never considered barriers to the Kamal path. The main point is for human beings to attain the love and insight that prevents them from making a mistake in choosing their destination. And so, they have no excuse for not following it.

> *What does a human being do with his life when he knows Thee?*
>
> *What does he do with his children, spouse and properties when he knows Thee?*
>
> *You make him fall madly in love with Thee, and give him the two worlds.*
>
> *But what does 'Thy' lover do with the two worlds when he seeks nothing but Thee?*
>
> *- Molana Rumi*

Countless people -due to their incorrect worldview that makes their companions their actual goal in life- lose their senses and become somehow sick when they lose their beloved persons.

As the final point in the mountain climbing metaphor, the mountaineer must sooner or later turn back from the top. Turning back is meaningless in the Kamal journey; however, similar to a mountaineer who is more experienced and ready to confront the problems in returning, the more a Kamal-seeker progresses, the more will he become mature and experienced, and the better will he perceive how to reach peace with others and appreciate them together as a group and union. Climbing high mountains teaches human beings to appreciate their companions. It makes them realize how precious the existence of each companion can be.

> *Let us appreciate each other*
> *Before we lose each other*
> *- Molana Rumi*

5. Absence of Knowledge, Understanding, and Perception of Worldly Love

God has manifested the entire universe by 'Love', and His love is the sole reason for their being in the universe. In other words, the starting step of Creation was based on love and all that followed had the same impetus and property.

> *On the first day of eternity when the ray of God's beauty was manifested,*
> *Love was created and forged the entire world.*
> *- Hafez*

Not only is God's love and mercy the one and only reason for their manifestations; furthermore, what gives human beings a different meaning from other creatures is again 'love'. The human being became the bearer (messenger) of love, whereas, all the skies and the earth refused to bear it.

> *The sky could not accept the responsibility,*
> *And the lot fell upon me, the madman of His love.*
> *- Hafez*

This way human being became the only creature who had the ability to understand and perceive Love, an ability that the other creatures utterly lack. It is true that all the divine creations have been created based on Love and that they float in it; however, except for human beings, none of them are aware of it and they cannot consciously enjoy it.

Thou! Saki![9] The angel doesn't know what Love is.

Request a glass of divine wine and pour the rose water on the human.

- Hafez

Or:

Thou! The angel, Tell the praise to God in front of the divine tavern door

The human nature has been leavened over there

- Hafez

In general, '*Adam*'[10] experiences love through three stages:

The first stage: In this stage, after '*Adam*' was prostrated [by the angles], he comprehended that the entire universe had been created for him. God even congratulated himself for his creation, and so, Adam focused on himself. After becoming aware of himself, he fell in love with himself. Hence, Adam experienced the first stage of love and was captivated by love for himself. And without paying attention to

---

9- The mystics have likened the Divine grace to drinking wine. The wine from His wine-jar of awareness and insight runs into man's soul and in addition to creating spiritual joyfulness and intoxication it also pours knowledge, awareness, insight, and love. In mystic language God is called 'The Server' (Saki) of wine. (Human From Another Outlook, M.A. Taheri)

10- What is meant by Adam here is not the prophet Adam. People collectively are the multiplicity of the existence of Adam, and the prophet Adam is one of them. In other words, the general truth of all people is a single being that is called "Adam" (Human Insight, Unity of existence, M.A. Taheri).

the recommendations, he drew close to the [*sole*] *tree of existence*[11] to experience it himself.

The second stage: At the present time, nearly all of us -as mankind- are experiencing this stage. At this stage we have a dual capability; we can fall in love with both ourselves and someone or something except ourselves. In other words, we fluctuate between our self-love and love for others until our love is shifted completely to others (apart from ourselves). As a result of which we find a manifestation of divine grace and will be free from self-centeredness.

A baby is born into this world in [a state of] self-love. Thus, their desires and motivations are all about fulfilling their needs. They even seek their mother because of their need to eat. Of course, without the sense of hunger they would not seek their mother and they could consequently not grow up to free themselves from selfishness after [spiritual] adolescence and through Kamal and transcendence.

The third stage: In the third stage, the human being completely focuses his love on others (except himself). This stage, in which love is turned towards the outside, is the stage of experiencing divine grace.

Mercifulness (Divine grace) = complete attentiveness to others = perfect love = mature love

The sun exhibits complete mercy in shining because it is not concerned about whom it shines upon or what it gains for shining! It never cares

---

11- If an observer from beyond time (the unipolar world) observes the Dipolar world, not only would he see the past, the future, and everything at a glance, but he would also see the roots of that world. Gradually, with the superimposition of all existing layers of beings onto one another, a tree form appears whose branches are all connected to one trunk, revealing that a connection, unity, and relation between all parts are in place. We call this tree the "sole tree of existence." From the beginning of his creation, Adam observed the landscape independent of time and perceived the "sole tree of existence." (Human Insight, Unity of existence, M.A. Taheri).

about receiving others' praise or hatred. It [just] shines! So does the tree which generously presents its fruits to others and never asks whom it feeds or what gifts they give in exchange. This is the characteristic of the mature love. In this experience the individual's attention is completely diverted to the outside and there is no sign of the 'self'.

We have to learn from the pupil of the eye
That sees the others, and not itself.

-Khaj-e- Abdollah Ansari

All the constituents of the universe are in their zenith of perfection (Kamal), but the difference between human being and other constituents is that others are not aware of their existence, Kamal or their capabilities. Humankind is aware of his existence and we knowingly move towards becoming merciful. However, except for humans no other creature is aware of their existence. For instance, the animals, plants and the sun do not know that they exist.

One of the experiences that we gain through the '*enna lellah va enna ilayhe rajeoon*' [*or ilayhe-rajeoon*][12] [symbolic] Halqeh (circle) is moving towards the '*names of God*' and perceiving them; such as moving towards mercifulness with awareness. Since '*all of us will return back towards Him*' and He is '*the merciful*', we are all moving towards His mercy. And even in our current life we can experience His mercy.

Worldly love has a role in attaining the stage of love that is the experience of mercifulness. Worldly Love is similar to a piece of cheese

---

12- We are travelling towards Him (God) through a pathway that '*returns us back to him*' or the path of *ilayhe-rajeoon*. This is an inherent movement towards Kamal and reaching oneness with Him. It includes moving from multiplicity to unity and from being needy to needless. This path is composed of various lives (stages) that each end with death and the next life (stage) subsequently begins. For instance, after dying in this stage [life on earth], the stage of '*space-free*' begins, and, after that, the stage of '*time-free and space-free*' follows. (*Human Insight*, The Dipolar world, M.A. Taheri)

put in front of a mouse hole to draw the mouse out. love for others is what brings humans out of narcissism (the first stage of love). Through this element and by moving away from one's self, human beings find God's love. In truth, loving another person becomes a means of helping the individual separate from himself and attain the experience of rapture and freedom from egocentricity.

> *While 'you' are present, God disappears*
> *'You' should disappear so that God appears*
>
> *-Asiri-Lahiji*

Thus, Worldly love is a factor that ultimately brings the individual to Divine love.

> *Love comes this way or that way*
> *Either way, it leads us towards Him in the end.*
>
> *-Molana Rumi*

In order to reach the highest degree of love we must proceed step by step through the stages. Eventually the individual finds the strength and capacity to tolerate the great Divine love.

> *Consider it a divine dispensation if you find any loss in worldly love,*
> *As figurative love will ultimately bring you Divine Love.*
> *A fighter gives a wooden sword to his son*
> *So he can learn how to fight and become an expert in battle*
> *Love is the human being's wooden sword*
> *In the end, through this love, he becomes merciful*
>
> *-Molana Rumi*

If a real sword is given to an unskilled fighter, he will certainly hurt himself or others. So, it is essential that the person first practices with a wooden sword before taking the real sword in his hands. Experiencing

Divine Love and nearness to God also require preparations. In each stage of the *ilayhe-rajeoon* circle this readiness is obtained to a certain degree. Adam[13] also obtains other preparations while moving on the *ilayhe-rajeoon* path that ultimately leads to meeting Rab[14] (God). In our current life, experiencing worldly love is one of the important factors for this purpose that is also called **figurative love**. God's theosophy decrees that by experiencing worldly love the human being mounts one of the steps of divine mercifulness and achieves its perception.

> *It was God's theosophy and destiny*
> *That we are enamored of each other*
> *-Molana Rumi*

The ability to experience love is one of the turning points of human creation. But in general, humans comprehend love as a type of captivity which enslaves the two sides in a worldly love. However, in the divine plan, [worldly] love is a means for experiencing 'worldly unity' and 'seeing only one' (perceiving oneness). When a lover sees nothing but 'one', nothing will distract the person from his/her beloved. And through love, the individual perceives oneness and becomes a [true] Monotheist.

Monotheism is the perception of God's oneness which is achieved through [attaining] the perception of the unity of divine manifestations or the perception of the 'unified body'[15] of the universe, and the perception of Adam. A part of this oneness is perceived through the worldly love's experience of oneness. Not only is the staggering design of human beings' ability for such love not aimless, it is also one of creation's masterpieces. The human being can benefit from the lesson

---

13- Please refer to footnote number 10.
14- For details please refer to 'Human being and Rab', Human Insight, M.A. Taheri.
15- In this perception, the universe and all its constituents are perceived as divine manifestations. Thus, the individual considers himself in connection and unity with all the universal constituents.

of unity learnt from this experience to move towards Kamal.

The soul who has fallen in love will never inspire evil.

-Molana Rumi

Here, worldly love means a kind of love that lacks logical profit-seeking and the lover does not love the beloved for his/her own benefits. Most people experience love advised by the *step of wisdom*[16] [rational love] instead of using the abilities of the [perfect] love that exists inside them. We can call such logical desire *'like'*, which is completely differed from the desire that is based on love. Affection based on the *step of love*[17] does not guarantee the individual's interests and it might even endanger the person's life. In truth, love is completely different from like, because like is based on the recommendation of logical reasoning, and most people's [experience of] love is in fact *'rational love'*. In this case, our wisdom suggests falling in love but it is mistaken for love.

What is reckless is love and not wisdom.

Wisdom seeks what it can benefit from.

-Molana Rumi

Even at times other factors might be falsely considered as love. For

---

16- The human being is always faced with two steps, the step of wisdom and the step of love (Eshq). The step of wisdom is the world of quantity and the world of tools. (For details refer to 'Human From Another Outlook', by the same author)

Wisdom continually opposes any action that does not bring tangible and material benefits, and where man wants to follow the heart, it obstinately opposes. One of the characteristics of wisdom is seeking a benefit, whereas the spontaneous characteristic of Love contains no benefit-seeking. ('Definition of Erfan (Mystical) Movement', Human Insight, M.A. Taheri)

17- The step of love is the world of ecstasy and enthusiasm, wonder and surprise, attraction and fascination, sacrifice and love, and the like. It is called the "Tool-free World." The occurrence of these situations depends on no tool, and each of the phenomena of the step of love occurs spontaneously and is not achieved by personal desire. (Human From Another Outlook, by the same author)

instance, a youth goes far from his/her parents for education. Because s/he is far from their support, the individual unconsciously feels an emotional vacuum and seeks a new support to replace the previous one. In this case, they might choose and fall in love with the very first person they meet to make up for [the support] they lacked. Obviously, the root of such love is logical and unconscious. If the individual's situation changes after a while and the person somehow finds their independence, the sense of requiring a support will diminish and lose its importance. Thus, they will be astonished that one day they expressed liking to that person, and feel that they had made a mistake in their selection. So, the person hesitates in his entire love and it all ends in separation.

In fact, if the reason for [rational] love disappears, the love will become unstable and will reach its expiry date because emotional tendencies that are a result of the wisdom's profit-seeking have an expiry date and may be replaced.

Some people, due to their active wisdom software and their not-used love software, have a poor ability to love. They think that all their problems can be solved through logical relationships. This is very dangerous for their emotional part of life and it usually results in serious failures. Many of these people think that wordly love is a kind of gamble. You may win or lose, and that if you lose in the gamble of love, all your life is ruined. A large number of them even felt regretful, depressed, pessimistic, etc. during adolescence when they failed in love. In general, we have rarely considered the purpose, reason, and philosophy of love and owing to the fact that all logical loves have an expiry date, a considerable percentage of people should expect failure and disappointment.

In creation, the application of the divine gift of love is to flourish us.

This blessing can bring the person growth and transcendence. However, in practice, misapprehension of love and not having perceived it on the *step of love* can lead to depression, [spiritual] fall, confusion or even different types of diseases. In the worst scenario, many people may commit suicide when they lose this gamble. In this way, the tremendous divine value is reduced to an extremely low and unpleasant anti-value.

All these problems occur because most people (especially the young generations who are more exposed to this invaluable experience at the beginning of their lives) do not have the necessary worldview, understanding and perception of worldly love. Therefore, we must teach and clarify the purpose and philosophy of this divine destiny. And it is better to begin the basics of this training from childhood by correcting their worldviews to avoid any future tragic events. For instance, it is necessary to train the basic concepts of the *step of wisdom* and the *step of love*. Denying the aforementioned problems does not assist in solving them. On the contrary, the solution lies in becoming equipped with the correct worldview about worldly love.

6. Absence of Knowledge, Understanding, and Perception of Peaceful Person

The state of the peaceful person is not one we can achieve only through good deeds. This state is obtained through perceptions that result in making peace with God, with the universe, with one's self, and with the others. It means that the peaceful individual is at peace with God, with every single constituent of the universe, with one's self, and with others, and has no conflict with any of them. Consequently, the individual's thoughts, actions and words are also formed on the basis of this internal and multilateral peace.

In other words, the *peaceful act* is an act that brings humans closer to peace. And the *peaceful individual* is a person who is at peace. Such an individual has overcome his internal conflicts and has freed himself from other conflicts. For the ordinary people who are moving on the path of Kamal struggling with different conflicts acts as brakes. However, a peaceful person -who is at peace- does not have such inner brakes to stop his transcendent movement, and his mental energy is not concentrated on dealing with such conflicts. Accordingly, the status of the peaceful person is the highest status that the individual can ever acquire.

When a person is striving towards conflicts, their being does not work in integrity. Hence, the brain orders the secretion of poisonous chemical hormones. In other words, the conflict factor is one of the poisonous factors that harm human's health and take away their inner peace. One of the disease causing factors in humans is striving towards conflicts and not being at peace.

It is necessary to explain that achieving the state of the peaceful individual can put an end to inner conflicts with anyone and anything. However, this does not prevent us from defending the right and opposing the wrong. In fact the peaceful individual stands against oppression dutifully and [at the same time] without any hatred and detestation, and he defends justice at all times.

So as was mentioned, we can categorize peace into four different categories that include: making peace with God, with one's self, with the universe and with others. Making peace with God is the easiest and making peace with the others is the hardest stage. In order of easy to hard [to achieve] the four stages include:

1- **Peace with God**

2- **Peace with the universe**

3- **Peace with one's self**

4- Peace with others

For more acquaintance with each of these four fundamental transformations that are acquired on the path of mystical movement, they are separately explained bellow.

1- Peace with God:

Almost all people are in conflict with God's theosophy and justice, because they expect divine justice and theosophy to make life events pretty much work in their favor and as they wish. Thus, whenever events are seemingly not in their favor, they assume that God has not delivered justice in their case and that worldly affairs are normally for the benefit of others. As a result, God's justice and His theosophy are denied and human's creation is considered futile.

'*Divine justice*' is in fact the laws governing the universe which uphold the rights of all particles of the universe. And '*divine theosophy*' is the way that this justice is carried out which is lawful and based on the *Law of Reflection*. According to this law, human beings receive the reward of their enthusiasm for negative or positive desires[18]. Knowing the *Law of Reflection*, the individual realizes how divine theosophy

---

18- Each moment every human being has a reflection from his being, resulting from his thoughts, words, and deeds. This reflection that can be positive or negative, is reflected into the upper realm and passes through a filter that evaluates the human being's capacity and capabilities. This filter determines an appropriate reflection, negative or positive, that conforms to the framework of justice [and the person's capacity], and subsequently refers this reflection to the positive or the negative network to be implemented on the individual. The reflection, when executed, first amplifies the individual's original reflection, and second, it brings about a positive or a negative awareness for the individual that is consistent with his original reflection. Consequently, it either truly guides the human being or misleads him. Thus, a stingy person is most likely to become more [and not less] stingy over time, a malicious person becomes more malicious, or the aware person becomes more aware. (Human From Another Outlook, M.A. Taheri)

works. Subsequently, they understand the divine justice and how each person plays a role in the plan of mankind's life, [serving] as a means for divine theosophy to be carried out. And why people come across one another and become means for testing each other.

Humans cannot analyze the events of life unless they have a correct understanding of the divine theosophy and the *Law of Reflection*; otherwise, every time an event happens that is seemingly against their benefits, they question a lot of things that is the cause of conflict with God.

Another subject that causes conflict with God is the lack of understanding and perception of the philosophy of '*worship*'. As a result, the individual questions: "Why do we have to say prayers?" or "Why aren't our life problems solved with worship?" and "Why doesn't God grant health to the sick in exchange for worshiping Him?"

Many of us mistakenly think that worship is a commodity through which the person trades with God, whereas the acts of worship are means of approaching God. They are assigned to increase the individual's certitude about the truths of the universe and to cause inner transformation and increase the individual's Kamal growth.

In each of the worship ceremonies, connection and communication with God has special importance, and it is by establishing such communication that worship becomes fruitful. Only in this state (of worship) will the individual perceive himself as the bearer of love, and understand his leading role and position. And the excitation of this love and adoration will make him eager to continue worshiping.

In this case, the person eradicates the false belief that worship is [carried out] based on God's need, or that it is a gift to God in trade for benefits and for the individuals' needs to be satisfied. Instead, in correct worshiping (that is performed with the correct worldview) there is neither any plea nor debt of gratitude (to God or other people).

In the rank of '*no plea*' or '*no gratitude*' there is no expectation. Thus, failure to fulfill one's desires does not cause conflict with God. Generally it can be said that worship is '*fulfilling one's mission as a worshipper*' which brings transcendence. If a person perceives this, not only will they not experience conflict with God regarding the reason of worship or why their intentions are not fulfilled; on the contrary, as a result of the love that the worship itself further and further enhances, they will become [more] engaged in worship.

> *The devout spent all his life desiring for heaven*
> *Hardly was he aware that heaven is having no plea*
> -Saeb-e Tabrizi

Worship is for human growth. But as explained above, a high number of those who worship expect God to fix their lives in return for their worship, to solve their problems in the shortest possible time, and to cure their illnesses and answer their prayers. They consider worship a kind of bribe to God that settles their debt to Him. And so, it is God's turn to provide the required facilities and to solve all their issues at once. However, since such expectations are against the philosophy of worship and they are not fulfilled in practice, most of these individuals become depressed the minute they face life issues. At times, even after years of worship, they suddenly turn their backs to God. They stop praying and experience conflict with Him. As a result of this conflict they develop various diseases.

If the human being gains the necessary awareness of the philosophy of creation they will understand [God's] justice, theosophy and the philosophy of worship and thus easily make peace with Him. The individual's unawareness makes him believe that God has oppressed him, and so, he objects God's theosophy and does not regard Him as just. Conversely, we are all created according to a grand and determined plan, and by passing through different stages of lives[19], we are moving towards a valuable goal.

This truth is only perceived through the *step of love* and the awareness of this magnificent plan. An individual, who achieves perception and illumination, on the one hand becomes familiar with the land of love and makes deep peace with Him through amorous relationship with God. Moreover, by becoming aware of His theosophy and justice, the individual becomes grateful to Him wholeheartedly.

All the different kinds of conflict with God -a few of which were mentioned above- are solved on the movement towards Kamal and through the perception gained on the *step of love*. Thus, the individual reaches inner peace with the God on high. It should be mentioned that the highest and most beautiful level of peace with God is achievable through the perception of '*An al-Haq*' (I am God)[20] which has a long explanation.

2- Peace With The Universe:

It is through perceiving the laws governing the universe that peace with the universe is fulfilled. If we consider the literal meaning of the word '*universe*,' it is a set of entities including the sacred nature of God[21] and all His divine manifestations. However, when we use this word

---

19- Refers to elaye-rajeoon movement.

20- This is a perception through which the individual understands his relationship with his Rab (God). Such a person will understand the truth that his Rab is his 'Kamal reached' self (at the end of the ilayhe-rajeoon circle that has responded positively to God's invitation). He will not regard himself a Rab in the conditions of this world (but only perceives it). ('Humankind and Rab', Human and Insight, by the same author)

21- This is the polarity-less and absolute truth. ('ontology', Human and Insight, M.A. Taheri)

idiomatically, universe means the divine manifestations only. In this book, the word *'universe'* is applied in this idiomatic sense, referring to the set of the divine manifestations.

Peace with the universe requires two transformations. First, the importance of each constituent of the universe is revealed, and the individual who is astounded by the deep relationship between these constituents becomes (indirectly) attracted to the universe's current of love (that has organized this grand set). Second, the person reaches the perception that they should not impose their personal desire on any constituent such as time or the heaven. What brings the individual to such peace is *'symphasis with universe,' 'symphasis with heaven'* and *'symphasis with time.'*

'Symphasis with universe' is a kind of harmony with the constituents of the universe. It results in the perception of the unity of the universe. Additionally, *symphasis with universe* is the perception of the connection, cohesion, and dependence of all constituents of the universe with one another that together create one [Unified] Body. Such perception reveals that no constituent can be excluded from this body.

> *If you remove a single particle from its place,*
> *The entire world will be damaged*

> *-Sheikh Mahmoud Shabestari*

Generally, the existence of every single constituent is meaningful in the context of other constituents. This is called the *'transverse continuity'* of all constituents with each other. Regarding time, *'time continuity'* is also significant. According to this continuity, every constituent is meaningful along its past and future and is [considered] inseparable from both.

'Interdependency of the constituents' is another truth showing that each

constituent has a role because of its dependence on other constituents, none of which will play such a role if separated. Sometimes, due to the change in the ecosystem, the type of the constituents or the nature of their relationship change. Nevertheless, the universe always remains balanced.

Each constituent of the universe has an '*existence code*' that varies with the set in which it is located. The existence code of anything [uniquely] belongs to that thing like the specific barcode of any commercial product. For instance, a liver cell has a role and activity in the liver that would not exist outside of the liver anymore. This means that, this cell has a existence code that will change if it is separated from its related set. Thus, the decline of this cell is different in its location from its decline out of this location (individual life). Based on the *continuity law*[22], the existence code of each constituent is retained in continuity with other parts of the set in which it is located and with their healthful consciousness. The constituent's decrease is subject to the total decrease of that set; therefore, becoming separated from the healthy set decreases the length of life.

The human being is also part of the set of the universe and, if not in accord and at peace with other constituents of this set; he will be mentally, psycheally and physically damaged and will have a shorter life. On the contrary, one type of human immunity (that is indeed the most important type of all) is 'immunity through love.' In case of love for the universe even facing pathogenic factors is barely risky. For instance, the intelligent relationship of pathogenic microorganisms with different people reveals that those who are more at peace with their external world and are less concerned with these contaminations

22- Please refer to chapter 3.

are healthier and they survive epidemics.

To complete this example, it can be noted that any child is born symphasic with nature. Comparing the health of a rural child who lives without hygiene with that of an urban child -who despite the hygienic care of his parents suffers from different diseases- reveals that the consciousness emissions resulting from the parents' thoughts and even from the society are effective in the baby's peace or conflict with nature, and that they have a determining role in the baby's health or illness. Therefore, it seems that rural people whose lifestyles are closer to the consciousness of the ecosystem suffer less from diseases compared to city dwellers.

'*Symphasis with universe*', other than causing harmony with the universe, has other consequences that are considered cognitive. One of these consequences is the perception of God's magnificence in each and every constituent of the universe. The person who achieves such perception sees the divine manifestation (which is nothing but beauty) in everything through his heart, and achieves the '*state of gratefulness*'.

The opposite of gratitude is blasphemy which means hiding the truth. An individual who ignores the sacredness of the constituents of the universe (divine manifestations) is a blasphemer, whereas gratitude means appreciating everything and accepting it as a divine blessing. The grateful person identifies and acknowledges His blessings and consciously and thankfully uses them.

Therefore, one can generally say that according with the universe and its constituents, and appreciating each single one of them indicate *peace with the universe*. Although this peace is not obtained as easily as peace with God, it is achievable through connection with Him and as a result of His grace.

3- Peace With One's Self:

An individual makes peace with themselves when they identify their position in the universe and achieve self-realization. Then, based on this awareness, they exercise sound and dynamic management of their personal power. For a better understanding of this subject, it is necessary to study the different kinds of conflicts with one's self.

The primary basis of conflict with one's self or other types of conflicts is the dipolarity of the human existence which provides the possibility for their test and growth. Each person has two classes of factors and tendencies; those relating to Kamal and those relating to anti-Kamal. These two have always been and will always remain to be part of the human beings' existence. In case of not controlling anti-Kamal tendencies, their inner factors will remain active; hence, peace with one's self does not occur.

Another major factor of conflict with one's self is any of the multiple tendencies that relate to the '*Foundation*' software[23] which accompany the individual from birth. Each one of these tendencies and their relevant reactions might be more dominant in any individual. This causes inner conflicts in itself.

This set includes '*reclusion-seeking*', '*superiority-seeking*', and '*affection-seeking*', which, respectively, cause escapist, aggressive and compromising reaction behaviors. The *reclusive person* wants to avoid any bother. And so, the slightest annoyance causes the individual inner confusion. The person who has *superiority-seeking* tendency endeavors to make others obey

---

23- Foundation determines the primary personality and the software-based character types of each individual. It is due to this software that even identical twins behave differently towards their surroundings from birth, and there may be certain personality characteristics in newborns that are entirely different from those of their parents (Psymentology, M.A.Taheri).

him. Thus, when encountered with someone who does not accept and obey their dominance, they feel defeated and frustrated. The weakness of the *affection-seeking* person is that they constantly need to be held in great affection by others, and any lack of affection or [the sense of] being neglected by others leads to their distress.

The important point is that in more psychologically sound characters there is balance between these three tendencies and the reactions relating to them.[24] Attaining perception and awareness, cosmic symphasis with universe and correcting one's worldviews all help create this balance.

In the above mentioned characteristics of the person's Foundation, the individual's criteria and worldviews have an important role in causing peace or conflict with one's self. Additionally, as experience shows, in the other types of conflict with one's self, the lack of awareness, false criteria and incorrect worldviews are the major causes of disorders. Examples of such conflicts are as follows:

• When the individual is not ready to encounter social, political, economic, and cultural conflicts, they easily lose their inner balance when they are confronting with such issues. In other terms, they suffer conflict with one's self.

• When the individual cannot discern between good and bad, and feels helpless, they both become confused at the time of decision and suffer conflict with one's self after their choice does not achieve the desired result.

• Without conformity and coordination between the individual's action and thought, the least damage they sustain is the increase of internal stresses which finally lead to psychosomatic diseases. One type of conflict of action and thought is the dual (two-faced) behaviors

24- The definition of character and sound character in the writer's view can be found in the book Psymentology, M.A.Taheri.

mentioned in the book 'Human from Another Outlook'[25]. As per the process explained in the book, such behaviors cause psychosomatic disease. These stresses indicate conflict with one's self.

• Those who are self-centered apparently seem to be at peace with themselves; however, narcissism highly increases the individual's vulnerability. Thus, contrary to what we imagine, such individuals suffer from intensive inner conflict.

• Those who find a large gap between their real state and their ideal character have conflict with one's self, and this conflict and their Defensive Psychological Response[26] can even make them go mad! For instance, many people who are in mental care centers and suffer from the

25- While interacting with the outside world events, an individual must often exhibit two-faced behaviors to better adapt to his environment (Two-faced behaviors compose a major part of our behaviors). As this behavior is not favorable or desirable for him, it can consequently lead to agitation, frustration, bottled up feelings, and so on, followed by the accumulation of a type of negative energy called the negative potential energy. When the quantity of such negative energy reaches a certain level, the individual will be taken to the High Court and goes through a one-way conviction. The reached [guilty] verdict is executed on the individual as a physical illness, which sometimes has no specific physical symptoms, yet one feels the pain and the related disabilities. As this type comes with no physical symptoms, the medical doctor would tell these patients that their problems are stress related, or more specifically, that they have psychosomatic illnesses.

26- The defensive self or the Defensive Psychological Response is one of the most important sections of the subconscious. It enables the person to adapt to the environment and considerably reduces momentary stresses and anxieties. However, this defense in the majority of cases does not follow logic and is a form of self-deceit and escaping from the truth, very similar to a mother who is defending her child [on the principle that the ends justify the means]. Therefore despite all its necessity, the defensive self often harms and creates loss for the individual. The defensive self defends a human being thoroughly and in all aspects, similar to a mother who in defense of her child would not consider many matters as she should, such as fairness and justice, righteousness or unrighteousness, and only thinks of getting her child out of the dangerous situation, so does the defensive self. In other words the defensive self acts like the friendship of a false (insincere) friend most of the time. (Human from Another Outlook, M.A. Taheri).

delusion that they are specific scientific, military and the like characters have the same experience. Such individuals' anxiety and confusion leads to Defensive Psychological Response and the consequent disorder that makes them believe they truly are their ideal and favored character. In fact, the defensive self (in charge of the Defensive Psychological Response) with the help of the body and cells' management (part of the Mental body)[27], cuts the connection between the Executing Self and the Ideal Self; thus, the individual considers himself the Ideal Self. For instance, in mental care centers we might have patients that believe they are apostles of the Savior [or Hitler, Napoleon ...] and are all considered to have lost their minds.

In addition to the above cases, there are also other similar examples of conflict with one's self. Whatever the case may be, the conflict-causing factors mentioned in each of these examples are barriers to peace with one's self. Controlling and managing all these factors necessitate an awareness and perception that is the cause of the individual's broad and deep self-realization.

> *I have many conflicts inside of me*
> *each one with their own opposite effects*
> *with them coming and going every moment*
> *how am I supposed to be at peace with others?*
> *See the armies of my conflicts*
> *Each at war with one another*

27- The Mental body is one of the countless bodies of the human being. It is a management that organizes different sections and consists of several subdivisions, and each subdivision in turn can be considered as a separate body. Mental body consists of: cell and body organization, human perception organization, data organization (the eternal data archives), memory and archive of the eternal data, memory management, data-arranging management (creating thoughts), cell and body management, and so on. (Human From Another Outlook, M.A. Taheri)

When you realize such a harsh war inside yourself
How can you waste your time fighting with others?

-Molana Rumi

In sum, there are a variety of potential [inner] conflicts in human beings, some of which include:

(1) **Fundamental conflict:** Good and evil

(2) **The primary conflict** that is born with us as part of our Foundation: 'affection-seeking', 'reclusion-seeking', and 'superiority-seeking'.

(3) **Conflict between the 'Executing Self' and the 'Ideal Self'**

(4) **Conflict between one's action and thought**

4- Peace With Others:

Conflict with others is the main barrier on the path of Kamal and in achieving the rank of the peaceful. If we consider the four mentioned aspects of peace as the four stages of the Kamal path, the most difficult to traverse is peace with others. It is therefore regarded as the main stage in achieving the rank of the peaceful.

There is only one way for resolving conflicts with others and achieving peace with them, and that is to achieve awareness and perceptions such as perception of the *magnificence of the Beloved*[28],

---

28- In the realm of love, there is a principle that serves as a valuable yardstick for recognition of being in love: 'The one in love finds the beauty and magnificence of the beloved faultless.' The Leyli and Majnoon story (an Iranian famous love poem) teaches this lesson clearly to man. In the story, their love became a word of mouth and everyone assumed how beautiful Leyli must have been to have made Majnoon so crazy for her love, to such a level that he wandered about in the plains and deserts. Therefore, everybody was curious to see her, and finally the king summoned Leyli to his palace. He wanted to see her, face to face, to see the beauty that had created such a great love. However, when the king finally met Leyli, he was amazed to find her quite an ordinary girl. Therefore, he told her, 'Then it is you that have caused Majnoon to

perception of *analhaq*[29], perception of the *unified body*[30], and so on. As a result of such perception, the individuals find the place of others in Kamal path and realize the dignity and sanctity of each constituent of the universe as a divine manifestation. This perception reduces their tension and conflict with others and brings them closer to the rank of the peaceful.

One of the differences between the human beings and other beings is that humans have no fixed and predetermined behavior and every second and based on their will, they can create new existential effects (such as thought, conduct and words). In other words, the human being is a creator within his own limits and capacities[31], and when communicating with other people, he exposes others to (his) diverse existential effects. Consequently, the differences of opinion, conflict of interest, annoyance, and misinterpretations create the opportunity for conflict between people.

Therefore, it is possible for a person to have realized the sacredness

---

[madly] wander about in the deserts, but you are not prettier than the others?!' In response, Leyli unveiled the great truth: "It is the way Majnoon perceives me that has indeed caused such a passionate love and it is his loving eyes that cannot see my flaws". Someone who has such eyes as Majnoon's can pass through both worlds easily as they cannot see any fault in them.

29- 'Baitollah' (the house of god) is exclusively used to refer to human being, given that it is the only place where in God has breathed the essence of His Spirit ('And I (God) breathed into him of My spirit' - Quran; Sura Al-hijr,Verse 29). Thus, we must approach other individuals' boundaries with total inviolability and sacredness, and no human being has the right of intrusion there. Anyone who reaches such perception has indeed reached the perception of 'AnalHaq' and is considered an intimate of the 'Baitollah.'

30- The world of unity is a world that is perceptual (needs to be perceived) in which an individual perceives the Unified Body of the universe. In this perception, the universe with all its constituents is perceived as divine manifestations. Thus, individuals consider themselves in connection and unity with all universal constituents.

31- Please refer to 'Stages of Universe and Reason', Human and Insight, M.A. Taheri)

of each constituent of the universe through the perception of the universe's unified body, and to have achieved the state of *'peace with the universe'*, but [at the same time] not to be easily freed from conflicts with other people. In this state, the truth that each individual is a divine manifestation becomes neglected and people lose their sacredness and respect in each others' eyes.

Nevertheless, when the person achieves the perception wherein he accepts everybody in their own place, he will not feel personal hatred and conflict towards them even if he regards their behavior as improper. And at the same time that he turns away from their false ways and worldview and even opposes them with the right approach, from within, he respects all other individuals as divine manifestations and is at peace with others.

The final point that requires special attention is that none of the four types of peace are attainable via advice and counsel, because peace is achievable on the *step of love* and advice and counsel are not applicable on this step. In order to accomplish this important task, an inner transformation is required that is not possible without His divine grace and mercy.

> *Me and advice! We have nothing in common!*
> *Oh Saki! Fill my soul with Thy divine wine*
> *-Molana Rumi*

7. Absence of Knowledge, Understanding, and Perception of Time (Asymphasis with Time)

One of the problems that lead to human beings' disease is absence of *time symphasis*. As will be discussed, this problem brings about distress, irritability, and nervousness, and physical, psycheal and mental diseases and many other issues in due course.

One of the results of moving along the mystical path is achieving *time symphasis.* In fact, in addition to this transcendental transformation, the individual also becomes aware of its importance and necessity. Generally, people try to dictate time. They desire time to pass as they wish; however, as one of the intelligent constituents of the material world, time reacts negatively against their compelling demand. Therefore, when a person wishes time to pass slowly, it appears to pass rapidly in their view, and when they desire it to pass rapidly, it passes so slowly that they think it has stopped or is hardly passing.

For instance, a prisoner desires the imprisonment time to pass more rapidly, but contrary to his wish, the more he desires, the more slowly time passes. To him 'one' single day may even seem like a week for the person outside prison as if time does not intend to pass. Other people who are free and who concurrently wish time to pass more slowly so that they can better handle all their affairs, [conversely] feel time pass so rapidly that noon arrives before they accomplish anything and the night falls in the blink of an eye. All the following days and nights pass just as rapidly.

While the second hand of all clocks goes forward equally everywhere and for all people, and even though the quantity of time is equal for everyone, both groups, either those who wish rapid time passage or those who desire slow time passage, are tormented by the way time passes and suffer from it. Such suffering results from imposing one's personal views on time, because according to a certain law of the universe, as a result of our internal tendency for the slow or rapid passage of time, we sense time against our expectations.

The quantity of time is always fixed; however, since people's feelings are variable (depending on the circumstances) we find the quality of time variable. Time is considered intelligent because its changes are regulated by the circumstances, and it seems that time behaves intelligently towards humans. For the same reason, we will encounter problems if we try to dictate to it. For instance, we have all well experienced that our insistence on rapid or slow passage of time causes us to feel it passing against our tendency. In fact, the human being has a variable sense of time.

In the mystical point of view, peace with all constituents of the universe including time is of utmost importance among all affairs. *Mysticism's* framework reveals the necessity of symphasis with time and presents the way of achieving it. In this state, the individual is in harmony with time and does not expect it to pass rapidly or slowly but is obedient and submissive to it. The important point is that only in this way we can enjoy time's blessings. Thus, one of the meanings of *patience* is being symphasic with time. A patient person is a person who is not dictating to the passage of time and is in harmony with it.

Furthermore, one of the barriers to the relationship between parts and the whole[32], and receiving awareness (inspiration)[33], is the lack of

---

32- Every individual (part) compared to the 'whole' is like every cell in a person's body compared to their whole. As a cell is unaware of the intelligent goals of its owner, every human being lacks the understanding of the purpose of creation without the contact with the whole, and it is likely that they would spend their life in a struggle for survival and make him/herself and others suffer from this ignorance. The prerequisite of the relationship between a constituent and the whole (the divine intelligence or the Interuniversal Consciousness) is 'submission'. ('Characteristics of the Erfani Movement', Human Insight, M.A. Taheri)

33- The human mind has limited ability to discover the truths, even using all its tools; however, the attempt to discover truths can be made possible through the tool-free step and by communicating with the whole and obtaining its endless and broad awareness.

time symphasis. Awareness and inspiration belong to the person who is at peace with time. Based on the enthusiasm which the individual has for acquiring awareness, the answer (awareness) is sent; however, similar to a parcel that is delivered to the householder only when they are at home, this awareness is given to the individual only when they are available at the present time. Otherwise, they are regarded as *absent* and miss the possibility of receiving the delivered message. In fact, when an individual expects time to pass rapidly, they move ahead of time, and when they want to stop time, they move behind it. In both cases, no inspiration or illumination happens and they are deprived of receiving [their] heavenly portion.[34]

Therefore, *Mysticism* increases mystical achievements by creating harmony with time because [both] receiving inspiration and the qualitative transformation of the human existence (gained through the connection of parts and the whole) depend on 'time symphasis', and are achieved as an infrastructural transformation in the *mystical* movement. In other words, *time symphasis* is one of the elevating factors in the path of Kamal, and the individual who has enthusiasm for transcendence realizes the importance of this harmony and discovers its howness and hence moves towards its fulfillment.

As discussed in the journey and destination section, the majority of people are not keen on traveling the life's journey (which is time-consuming), and tend to have time collapsed to reach their destination. Thus, man is the killer of '*time*' and one of the constituents that will

---

What is regarded as awareness is the information related to the truth that is obtained by the ultra-mental receptors and are not made or discovered by the mind. ('Achieving Kamal Awareness', Human Insight, M.A. Taheri).

34- Heavenly blessings include inspiration, illumination, perception, transcendental transformations, and whatever is needed on the path of Kamal. In sum, the fulfillment of heavenly affairs requires the individual's enthusiasm and submission.

testify against him is 'time'.

In other words, humans often oppose the passage of time by [only] thinking about reaching their destination. Like so time is ignored, and based on [universal] laws it intelligently stands against the human being and disappoints him by not allowing the individual to optimally benefit from life. And so, the individual resists against the *elayhe-rajeoon* movement which is [considered] an oppression to oneself because time [in turn] reacts against this resistance and practically limits the individual's opportunities.

I swear by the time, surely, the human is in a (state of) loss

- Quran; Sura Al-Asr, Verse 1-2

One of time's reactions is its reaction to the human being's excitement and inner worries. It seems that with the generation of false excitement, the sense of time also becomes faster. Namely, with the increase in false emotions and stresses resulting from the progress of technology and promotion of mechanized life, we feel rapid time passage. For example, fifty years ago, people had a more stretched sense of time. That is, a day was felt longer than it is felt today and obviously in fifty years time, the passage of time will be felt much quicker than today.

In addition, the sense of time is shorter in the city than in the village. The reason for this phenomenon is that the level of excitement and rush is higher in the city; thus, the urban population feels time pass much faster than those living in the village. The city rush and hurry indirectly tends time not to pass. People's rush shows that they want to have more time to spend and this is a type of dictating to time, and so, time fights against these demands. However, people living in rural areas are not in a rush and they dictate less to time compared to city dwellers. The villagers are less likely to think that time should pass quickly; consequently, they have an overall longer feeling of time.

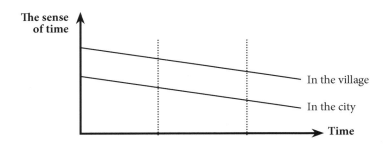

8. Absence of Knowledge, Understanding and Perception of the heaven (Asymphase with the heaven)

People have long complained about the oppression of the heaven:

> *O' thou heavens! All demolitions come from your animosity*
> *Oppression is your longstanding practice.*
> *O' thou Ground! If your heart were excavated,*
> *There are many jewels in your heart.*
> *-Khayam*

Many people desire to change the universe and the heaven, but feel depressed because they cannot change them:

> *You want to change the heaven,*
> *But the heaven never accept the changes*
> *-Roodaki Samarghandi*

These complaints prove that the heaven does not behave according to mankind's wishes, yet people persist in imposing their demands and endless wishes on the universe and everyone is extraordinarily entangled with it. The human being's greed and insatiable hunger plague them endlessly and they are imposing their right or wrong desires on the heaven all the time. This useless struggle is one of the factors that create physical, psycheal and mental diseases. Many have experienced how an unfulfilled wish can create depression and prepare the grounds for other diseases.

For earthly wishes to be fulfilled, rather than focusing on them, they should be set free. Otherwise, they become more unachievable. The common expressions that reflect the thousands of years of human experience show that we should never be enslaved by our wishes. For instance, the proverbs meaning 'problems occur to people in trouble' or 'turning up like a bad penny' and the like that are common amongst different nations and people, and nobody denies them or considers them superstitions, reflect the human beings' [common experience of] disappointment with the fulfillment of issues that they insist on or the things that they try to avoid. Thus, it seems that the heaven also react against human beings based on intelligent principles. In other words, the heaven behaves based on [universal] laws.

- Here the heaven, the cosmos and similar terms refer to the 'Universe.'

A 'wish' refers to a desire that is not practicable at the moment. Because if it were possible to achieve or if it had been achieved, we would not call it a 'wish' anymore. Actually, a 'wish' is a kind of desire that is currently impossible to achieve. In general, the fulfillment of a will or an earthly wish is a function of the *law of [worldly] effort*, and a person can gain nothing unless he works for it.

> *...that man can have nothing but what he strives for.*
> -Quran; Sura An-najm, Verse 39

In addition to expedience and effort, other factors are required to fulfill a wish that include:

(1) Principle of achievability

(2) Principle of no mutual conflict between desires

(3) Principle of justice

(4) Principle of no conflict between one's desire and the laws of the universe

(1) Principle of Achievability

Achievability means the chance and possibility of a wish fulfillment that depends on various factors. For instance, if all the people of a country wish to become rich immediately and without having a predefined plan for the country's economic growth, the Central Bank cannot fulfill such public demand because, in exchange for the country's banknotes and its currency rate, an amount of gold and reserves exist in the Central Bank without which money is valueless. This reliable backing cannot be attained without a plan, work and effort; thus, the dream is nothing more than a desired objective and not the direct causing agent. So, wishing and wishful thinking cannot make all the classes rich because it is contrary to the principles of economics and banking. Nevertheless, if considered as a motivating factor, it acts as a positive factor in the pursuit of the dream which subsequently leads to greater effort and achieving results.

In other words, the currency of a country which flows among the different classes of its people has a fixed rate. Without doubt if some people have a higher amount of this fixed money, others lose it proportionately. Therefore, the dream of everyone becoming rich is not achievable without a precise economic plan -that can bring remarkable economic growth to the country- and mass efforts (which depend on the effort and positive thinking of the public). In addition, to achieve such a wish, it is essential to devise a framework for fair distribution of wealth among different social classes. For this reason, only imagining becoming rich does not make everyone wealthy.

We will give another example to discuss the [principle of] achievability of wishes. Throughout history, millions of people wished to travel to the moon and to walk on its surface, but in reality how many had their wish fulfilled? The percentage of such people is almost zero because compared to the millions of mere wishers only a few have been able to walk on the moon which is considered insignificant. Thus, for the millions who wish so today, the achievability is zero. However, traveling to the moon might become common in future similar to the dream of flying in the sky that despite never coming true for billions of people is something commonly achievable today and no one thinks of it as a '*dream*' anymore.

(2) The Principle of No Mutual Conflict Between Desires

Obviously, it is not possible for all people to achieve all they wish for because many of the individuals' desires conflict with other people's. In fact if all wishes were to be fulfilled, mankind would face many problems since many of his worldly desires and wishes are in conflict with one another.

Consider these simple examples. At the same time that a farmer desires rain, others who are heading out on a picnic wish for sunny weather to better enjoy their time out. Or people driving at the end of a lane of traffic, moving slowly towards a green traffic light, want the light to remain red for the other roads until they cross the intersection. In conflict, the people stopped behind the red traffic light want it to change quickly to green.

In both of these examples, the [opposite] desires of the two groups cannot be fulfilled by the heaven. In the more obvious second example, if the heaven fulfills the demand of one group, they have acted against justice [and unfair to the other group]. Thus, it is impossible to fulfill the desires of all the above groups [in either situation at the same time].

(4) The Principle of No Conflict between Demands (One's Desires) and the Laws of the Universe

This is another principle that prevents the fulfillment of all desires. The laws relating to the foundation and management of the universe have created an order that cannot be disturbed by any will or wish. If fully comprehended, it leads us to never expect it to change as per our personal desires. Natural events such as earthquakes, lunar and solar eclipses, lightning, storms, and the like, demonstrate that despite people's fear that arose from their ignorance in the past, they still constantly recurred. And people's wish to stop them from happening could not prevent or eliminate them. Such natural events undoubtedly occur in accord with the universe's laws, and human desire exerts no control on such phenomena. It all points to the conclusion that nothing can violate these principles.

Some people ignore these principles and try to popularize wishful thinking and introduce the heaven as obedient to the influence of people's words and thoughts. On the contrary, through careful consideration of the provided examples and explanations it is realized that fulfilling all demands and wishes is impossible. We also find that not only are the heaven not appointed to follow human's desires but it always act against a person's persistent entreaties [that contradict the laws of the universe].

Therefore, we should not be haunted by our dreams and dictate to the heaven because the consciousness that rules the heaven stands against the fulfillment of such entreaty. Instead, after briefly skimming one's worldly wishes (which can sometimes be a factor for effective actions), the mind should be released from them forever as if they never existed. Worldly desires that are of least consideration and are set free will be fulfilled easier than those we have hung on to [in our mind].

In other words, if after a brief attention (Nazar)[35] on our wishes, we clear them from our mind, we will not encourage the heaven and the universe to go against their fulfillment. This way we also show that our minds are not slaves to our worldly demands. If the mind obsesses over distant and unreachable worldly wishes, they will consume all our mental energy and after a while, confuse us in a way that we cannot think rationally even about the simplest life problems.

Furthermore, the pest of wishful thinking (desiring our wishes to be fulfilled spontaneously and effortlessly) prevents us from finding solutions, managing, and taking innovative measures. Instead, it turns us to a wishful thinker that constantly fantasizes about finding a treasure, obtaining huge wealth from the heavens, and the like, and departs us from reality.

It should be noted that contrary to worldly demands, *spiritual wishes* should capture the entirety of the individual's existence and mind, and shape them. Because even the human behavior, speech and thinking eventually take the shape of what we have on our minds.

> *If you think about a flower, you are a flower,*
> *And if you think about a nightingale, you are a nightingale.*
> *You are a constituent and God is the whole.*
> *If you think about the whole during the day, you will be the whole.*
>
> -Ja'ami

Thus, how amazing is it for the human being to take the shape of the divine thought instead of a non-spiritual desire. Yet many people have

---

35- Please refer to footnote number 6, chapter 2.

taken a materialistic shape, following nothing but their non-spiritual (worldly) desires.

> *So long as you seek jewels, you are a jewel.*
> *So long as you seek daily bread, you are bread.*
> *If you realize this secret point you find*
> *Everything you seek, you are.*

> -*Molana Rumi*

One of the goals of the world of mysticism is for individuals to focus on spiritual desires and constantly think about attaining transcendence and Kamal. If the sufficient enthusiasm for taking the Kamal pathway emerges in people and if their entirety of existence is captured in that pursuit, their worldly desires that are the cause of dictatorial attitude towards the heaven will eventually vanish.

Furthermore, when people are symphasic with the heaven (harmony with the universe and perceiving the way of accompanying with it), as a result of the transformation that takes place, the individual can completely release their non-spiritual wishes after considering them briefly (*Nazar*). In addition, this symphasis and harmony is the infrastructure upon which they experience more profound transformation.

In the mystic world, individuals reach the rank of 'submission' and among all their will and wishes they seek the divine one granted by God and determining Kamal. They finally reach the status where they say:

> *One desires pain and one desires remedy.*
> *One desires joining and one desires separation.*
> *Of the pain, remedy, joining, and separation,*
> *I desire what He desires.*
> -*Baba Taher*

Chapter 3

The Laws of the Universe and the Principles Governing It

1. The Law of Relativity

One of the laws ruling the universe is the *law of relativity*. This law shows the relativity of phenomena and their lack of absoluteness. For a better understanding, we can ask a few sample questions and examine their answers:

-Is it harmful for humans to consume rat poison?

-Is it beneficial for humans to consume vitamin A?

-Is earthquake good?

-Is lightning bad?

-Is the devil evil?

Generally, our answers to these questions are different from answers based on the *law of relativity*. Human beings constantly face a high number of such questions and their related minor and major issues. In such case, if the 'relativity perspective' has not become part of the individual's worldview, they can commit fundamental mistakes. Three examples of relativity worldview are as follows:

A. The relativity of good and bad

B. The relativity of ownership

C. The relativity of ugly and beautiful

A. The Relativity of Good and Bad

If asked whether the devil is good or bad, what would we answer?

Without considering the *law of relativity*, the answer would be that evidently and for certain devil is evil. When we say 'for certain' it means that the existence of the devil has no benefit whatsoever. The human being generally has an absolutistic point of view, and as will be discussed, they are very fragile for this very reason. However, from the *'relativity perspective'* and considering the truth behind each phenomenon, the lack of absoluteness of good or bad is proved and a more transcendent worldview is gained.

For example, based on the *'relativity perspective'* the answer to the above question is that without the existence of anti-Kamal factors [reaching] Kamal would not be valuable, and it is through the existence of the devil and defeating it that human beings can reach transcendence. If Satan did not exist, overcoming what obstacle and reaching which Kamal peak would be the reason for the human beings' divine transcendence?

In fact, the devil is a tool for putting humans to the test and it is considered a touchstone for measuring the degree of their purity. In other words, we can be assured of our proficiency in Kamal and divine transcendence if we are faced with the devil and successfully pass his arranged tests. [Only] this way, the human being's movement is valuable. So, the existence of the devil plays a role in our Kamal and if there was no devil, no one would seek God.

Everything that has been created is grace and has its own benefit.

The world is like the hair, mole, eyes and eyebrows [of the Beloved]
Every constituent is good in its own place
-Shabestari

Furthermore, if we consider Satan as the pure evil, it will be the creator and origin of evil himself. Thus, pure good must also exist as the creator of good. From the perspective of a person who believes in God, the creator of good can be nothing except 'God' Himself. From this viewpoint, Satan (the creator of evil) is versus God (the creator of good); and this absolutistic point of view about Satan is belief in duality and evident polytheism.

The next question mentioned above was: 'Is earthquake good or bad?' People would widely answer that earthquakes are absolutely bad. However, from a *relativity perspective* and considering earthquakes' *truth of existence[1]*, the answer is that if there were no earthquakes, there would be no human beings. At first, this answer might seem extremely weird and unreasonable but with a little thought we realize that it is indeed true. The emergence of dry lands on planet Earth is owing to two phenomena; earthquakes and volcanoes. Without dry lands, no human being could exist, and if the Earth had remained under water it would not be possible for the human beings to live on it. So, the grace of earthquakes and volcanoes made it possible for humans to step onto earth.

Also, without the grace of thunder there would be no life on Earth because thunder on the one hand charges the rain-bearing clouds and creates rain which is the basis of life of land creatures on Earth. On the other hand, it forms the ozone layer by converting oxygen (O_2) into ozone (O_3). Without the existence of the ozone layer, living on Earth would not be possible and living things would not be protected from the harmful radiations of space. In other words, without thunder the harmful radiations from space would not allow any life on earth. However, from another perspective, thunder might well be considered

---

1- For definition of 'truth of existence' please refer to 'the law of order and disorder' in the same book.

dangerous, destructive and frightening. Accordingly, nothing can be judged from one angle only, because the human worldview might be independent from the *law of relativity* and they might judge things based on barely a few of its advantages or disadvantages. As a result, such worldview will be incorrect and immature.

Now, to understand the common worldview we could ask: 'Is eating rat poison good for human health or bad?' The majority of people would answer that rat poison is certainly harmful to human health. However, rat poison or white arsenic is the main substance for the treatment of sexually transmitted diseases. Its discovery goes back to an incident a century ago. At that time a young man from Turkey realized he was suffering from a venereal disease. Due to the lack of any available treatment, he decided to commit suicide and so he ate some rat poison. However, to his surprise not only did he stay alive, but his symptoms were also relieved! He immediately reported this to German doctors who examined the incident. This finally led to the production of sexually transmitted disease medicines.

By studying these and other examples we conclude that absolute bad does not exist and whatever the almighty God has created is grace, and if examined in its own place, everything has at least one benefit for which it has been created. Hence:

> *There is no such a thing as absolute bad in the world*
> *Badness is relative, you should know*
> *There is no poison, nor sugar in this world*
> *One has no leg, the other has no joints.*
> *-Molana Rumi*

There are also cases that most people evaluate as absolute good. For example if we ask: 'Is vitamin A good or bad?' some would quickly answer that it is good and beneficial. But high injection of vitamin

A can lead to the individual's death. Thus, defining it as good or bad depends on the person's need and the recommended dose.

In general, good or bad, usefulness or harmlessness of a subject depends on the place, manner and level of use. Thus, we cannot rely on a prompt and superficial judgment and give opinions accordingly. We need to properly explore and examine all the contributing factors and not leave any dimension unrevealed as it can create incorrect understanding and judgments. We also need to take into consideration that everything is ruled by the *law of relativity* and that nothing can be discussed with an absolutistic approach. If we look at the constituents of the universe from such a viewpoint we realize:

> **Nothing has been created in the universe except grace.**

Becoming aware of this law is an important factor that helps resolve our conflict with God. People object the creation of anything that is [apparently] not profitable for them. But, if they seek the truth behind its creation, they will definitely discover unknown reasons that are beyond their imagination. This will consequently resolve their conflict with God.

One of the reasons that drive the human beings towards the *world of multiplicity*[2] is '*absolutism*'. For instance, we used to have many friends. And if we look back on the reasons behind our separation from either

---

2- The world of multiplicity is the world in which individuals are separated from each other to such an extent that the world of each individual is entirely limited to themselves. Such a person does not recognize [anyone] outside the self and only takes themselves into account, and is only concerned about maintaining their earthly and material life and personal benefits. This process finally results in a struggle with one's self, and personal conflicts peak. In the world of multiplicity, no two people can tolerate each other (Halqeh Mysticism, M.A. Taheri).

side, we realize that the main reason was *'absolutism'*. In most cases, as long as everything about the person was just right we enjoyed their friendship but after viewing an undesirable behavior in the individual, we generalized it, judged them absolutely and avoided further contact with them. In other words, we changed our minds all of a sudden and abandoned them. Thus, we digressed from [*the world of] unity*[3] and fell into [*the world of] multiplicity*. While:

> *Each flower has its thorn*
> *The only flawless flower is God.*
> -*Parvin Etesami*

In the *'relativity perspective'*, since everything is viewed as relative and not absolute, the individual does not seek absolute and flawless good. In regard to others, he accepts that besides their good points and virtues, they might also have faults which are quite normal. Of course, this does not mean that the existence of faults is approved. Evidently, we need to take action to correct our faults. Meanwhile, in reality and in practice, humans still show unreasonable and incorrect behaviors, and if we shut our eyes to others' virtues, people will not be able to socialize anymore and everyone would be necessarily forced to isolate themselves from others. Thus, no two people will be able to live together.

This is a clear example of the *world of multiplicity* in which no two people can tolerate each other. Perceiving the *'relativity perspective'*

3- The world of unity is a world that is perceptual (needs to be perceived) in which an individual perceives the Unified Body of existence, and the universe with all its constituents are perceived as divine manifestations. Individuals with a perception of the world of unity, consider themselves in connection and unity with all universal constituents. The purpose of Halqeh mysticism is to help people reach Kamal and transcendence; a movement from the world of multiplicity to the world of unity. All efforts are for bringing people closer to each other, and any factors that separate people and create division among them is avoided (Halqeh mysticism, M.A. Taheri).

helps us not to fall into multiplicity and not to suffer the consequences of the '*absolutism*' incorrect worldview and the illnesses and spiritual and material losses that follow. Thus, when coming across people's first fault we will no longer forget all their virtues, nor suffer multiplicity and diseases as a result of '*absolutistic point of view*'.

According to a certain principle, nothing has been created without purpose and benefit, and without helping humans in a way. Thus, in processing information and analyzing events, a correct '*relativity perspective*' must be applied. Such worldview reduces the individual's conflict and prevents them from rapidly moving towards multiplicity. It solves conflict with others that is the greatest obstacle on the path to Kamal and facilitates movement towards [the rank of the] peaceful individual.

B. The Relativity of Ownership

If we ask ourselves: 'Am I the owner of my hands that are at my service?' Or, 'Am I the owner of the car that I have purchased because of its ownership papers?' What would the answer be? Do we believe that our hands, feet, eyes, teeth, hair and all the different parts of our existence belong to us?

Our definite response to these questions would be 'yes'. But, if we go to a hospital and go through the patients' records, we will see that many people might have lost an eye, leg, arm, and the like which they owned until an hour ago. Or, others had a child, spouse, sister, brother or parent who are lost today. And if we go to the emergency room of a hospital, we will find many people who have lost their beautiful face in a minor accident in seconds. Their beauty has vanished in a way that they could not have ever imagined. Although they might have previously been very proud of their beauty but now they hide themselves from the eyes of others.

Additionally, if we go to police stations we realize that many people owned cars, jewelry, expensive furniture and belongings which have been stolen. If we go to fire stations, we see that many who owned a house have lost all their property in a fire and presently they do not even have a place to sleep.

It may seem that human beings at least own their knowledge. However, many people who boastfully talked about their high level of science, knowledge, intelligence and talent, have lost it all in a small accident such as a concussion. Others have lost their memory in an accident and now have nothing to brag about.

Based on the fact that every person may lose all their possessions and abilities in an instant, what do we [certainly] own? And as an owner how long is this ownership valid?

With close attention we realize that despite humans' apparent ownership and the documents that prove it, the truth is that they own absolutely nothing and their ownership is only until further notice. This is in accordance with the 'relativity of ownership', based on which, human beings are considered owners only until further notice. Their authority is temporarily lent to them and it can end any single minute. The true owner is God (*God to whom belongs all that is in the heavens and the earth*)[4] and whatever humans own are relative.

Not being equipped with this worldview exposes human beings to anxiety, stress, depression and illness, and is one of the major reasons behind illnesses. So, without correcting our worldview, each of us could be exposed to a paralyzing shock at any given moment. For example,

---

4- Quran; Sura Nesa, Verse 126.

when someone steals our car, not only have we lost our car but we have also become ill. Therefore, without a steady worldview on the '*relativity of ownership*' the damages that we endure are multiplied.

In summary, the highest power the human being can achieve is the power to lose. The worldview of '*relativity of ownership*' gives us the capacity and power to lose, because the heaven does its job and continuously takes away. However, the important issue is how we view the loss.

C. The Relativity of Ugly and Beautiful

If the human being was to be taken out of the material world, ugliness and beauty would lose their meanings. In truth, the universe has no definition for ugliness and beauty on its own. The human being is the one who gives the universe its meaning and defines and interprets it. Otherwise, ugliness and beauty always coexist in nature without any objection.

> *Do not focus on the peacock's feather, see also its feet*
> *So your vision doesn't mislead you.*

> *-Molana Rumi*

If we appreciate the beauty of the peacock's feather, we should also appreciate its feet. This prevents an unsound understanding and does not allow us to digress from the truth of the universe's laws, and expect everything to be absolute beauty or absolute ugliness. Beauty and ugliness coexist in the universe; flowers come with thorns and the [beautiful] feather of a peacock comes with its feet, but their combination forms nothing but natural beauty.

Another worldview that causes illness in human beings is '*absolutism*' in evaluating beauty. In fact, through such perspective, the individual expects absolute beauty in God's creations; whereas, absolute beauty with practically no ugliness does not exist in any constituent of the universe. If this issue is not taken into account, everything might be considered as pure ugliness through the eyes of the individual. Consequently, the individual is deeply bothered. However, beside a flower, there will be thorns and this *relativity perspective* about beauty and ugliness makes the human being comprehend that next to beauty, there could exist ugliness and next to ugliness, beauty.

One of the consequences of understanding and perceiving this issue is its [effective] role in the individual's health. By accepting the *law of relativity* and the principle of non-absoluteness we can become free from the illnesses that result from stress. The lack of awareness of the *law of relativity* leads to stress and the subsequent physical, psycheal, mental and psychosomatic illnesses.

As we roam in the garden of the universe's mysteries and we decode its secrets and become aware of the unity of the material world, we realize that it is beauty throughout. In other words, through observing the garden of the universe and by breaking the spectacles of 'absolutism', we will be able to view the unity that governs it; which is another beauty in itself. Furthermore, the understanding and perception of such unity is the basis for perceiving the greatness of the divine plan. If a person reaches certitude about it, they will be able to observe the beauty engraved in the background of this astonishing plan.

> *Life is beautiful; open your eyes to it.*
> *Ramble around the garden of the universe's mysteries.*
> *Whoever views His beauty*
> *Breaks his pessimistic spectacles*
> *If you reach the light of certitude,*
> *Even the ugly will appear beautiful.*
> *-Molana Rumi*

2. The Order and Disorder Law

By designing a set of questions about order in the universe and studying their answers, we can understand one of the universe's laws and benefit from it in our lives. For this purpose, we have to answer questions such as: When looking at the sky, do we see order or disorder? And are the stars arranged in order or disorder? When we look at the forest, do we see order or disorder? Is it true to say that the sky, forests, and other natural phenomena consist of both order and disorder?

In order to answer these questions, it should be explained that any phenomenon in the material world is like a coin with two faces: one face **"Reality of Existence"** and the other face **"Truth of Existence."**

Reality of Existence:

Existential reality of every constituent of the universe indicates that it exists; it has taken place, happened or occurred whether or not we know the cause and howness [and quality] of its occurrence. Reality of existence either is observable, recordable and measurable, or exerts an effect on the environment. It may also display a combination of these characteristics. For example, [the 'being' of] a piece of stone is real whether or not we know how it has been created, because it has evidently come to existence. Some phenomena have reality although we are not able to perceive (see or feel) them with our five senses. For instance, we cannot see or touch infrared light, nevertheless it has reality, and we can discover it with the aid of some equipment, measure and even use it [in practice].

Truth of Existence:

The truth of existence is the quality, the reason, and the manner of existential reality and is achievable through discovering and examining such issues as follows:

1- The reason of existence and the manner of occurrence:

For example, what is the 'cause' of a stone's creation? [Why has it been created?] Or how and through what factors has the universe come into existence?

2- The plan (purpose) of existence and the hidden aspects of existential reality:

Any reality happens following a plan and design [plan of being]. Thus, by verifying those hidden aspects of each reality, one can become aware of and examine the reality's plan and purpose of being. For example, we can realize for what purpose has the human being come into existence? Or what is the philosophy of the universe's creation? (The reason of its creation)

3- The quality of existence:

The existential truth examines the howness and quality of existence of a reality in relation to a base point and analyzes it very closely. For example, having a base point, we can investigate whether a given reality truly exists [in the outside world] or it is an illusion. For instance, the reflection (image) of an object in the mirror has no existential truth because the image is virtual (illusory) in relation to the object. However, the image has existential reality [because it has come into existence through the mirror]. Therefore, it is possible for an entity in the universe to have an existential reality and at the same time not have an existential truth compared to its origin. And vice versa, an entity might not have a reality for us, but it can have existential truth (proving their reality), as does infrared light that is not considered real through naked eyes. However, because it can be detectable via special equipment it is no longer unreal. In other words, based on the detection equipment that is our naked or non-naked eyes we can say whether something has existential truth or not.

Another example is the aura surrounding each human being. As it is not visible to the naked eyes, for many years it was considered not to be real and in fact a superstition. However today that the aura is finally visible through Kirlian photography, no one can say that it lacks [existential] truth. Consequently, existential truths help us explore the unknown, realize their reality, and not consider them unreal anymore.

Now, when we look at the sky, the reality is that the stars are randomly arranged without any order and it appears that there is no principle behind their arrangement. Or when looking at a natural forest we see absolute disorder; whereas, if we carefully look at an artificial and man-made forest we see that all the trees are arranged in order and placed at certain distances. Therefore, if man was to design the sky, mountains, forests and other constituents of nature, all of them would have an orderly layout. Conversely, principles such as symmetry or any other principle that reminds man of order are naturally not viewed in the layout of such constituents.

In addition, when we seek the truth of above phenomena and study behind their scenes, we realize that behind their completely disordered appearance, there lies strict order and that they are directed by extremely precise and orderly principles. Therefore, we can say that the reality of the material world is based on disorder while its truth is based on order, or in other words:

> **"The universe is made of order and disorder."**

Application of the Order and Disorder Law

Since the universe is based on both *Order & Disorder*, it is said that *Order & Disorder* is one of the laws governing the universe. By understanding this law one can correct his/her worldview on the establishment of order in life, and consequently prevent the damages that are easily eliminated this way.

Take the case of a piece of string hanging from one's pocket, or a person's coat collar not neatly tucked, or a picture frame or a clock hung tilted on the wall of the waiting hall. How many people, being exposed to such cases, feel nervous and decide to undo this disorder or even get extremely nervous if correcting it is not possible? What is the actual link between an individual's psycheal or nervous system function and a picture slanted on the wall? How is it that the defects in our surroundings cause us stress and illnesses in the end?

As previously discussed, the information related to events and external occurrences pass through a world-viewing filter, and it is due to this filter that everyone is not equally affected when encountered with the same situation. The impact rate of each encounter depends on the predefined framework of this filter. Therefore, due to the lack of knowledge, understanding, and perception of worldview principles, most of us often experience tensions that consequently poison the body and cause spasm or other side effects. For instance, many women are obsessed with their everyday chores and housework, and are poisoned by [untidiness and] disorderliness.

Indeed, the main cause of a great number of our problems and diseases is not having studied the [symbolic] *'Book of Existence'*, and our unawareness of the *Order & Disorder* that forms the universe. Even though experiencing disorder is an inevitable part of life, and although complete and absolute order is not at all attainable, we never welcome disorder. Similarly, we are not inspired by nature's *Order & Disorder* although its never-ending and never-boring beauty is due to *Order & Disorder*. Indeed, the universe is made from *Order & Disorder*.

Our presupposed arrangements are a game of our mind. Our minds have become habituated to the frameworks invented by ourselves, and for this reason, if something is outside such framework it brings us discomfort and tension. Furthermore, the more we design our surrounding based on this mental pattern, the more intolerable it becomes to cope with the slightest disorder. Take the example of a luxurious house in which every piece of furniture is well-organized. In case of the slightest trace of untidiness we realize it without delay, and we experience spasm for a few minutes which threatens our peace. Conversely, in a cottage house that is not designed on order, disorderliness does not upset us or create any tension. So, despite its disorderliness, we can comfortably repose in it.

In a rural cottage there is no sign of orderliness, symmetry or systematic colors and the like. But, in an urban house everything is in a framework of orderliness, symmetry, concord of colors, and so on, and the slightest mess in the set immediately engages the mind and wastes its energy. For instance, if the walls, surfaces or doors are slightly mal-shaped, the mind focuses on it in torment. Whereas, in the case of a rural cottage which is designed based on [unsystematic] disorderliness, even the deformed walls, doors, stairs, and roofs are barely noticeable and they do not waste one's mental energy. That's why; only in a rustic ambiance can the individuals truly enjoy mental relaxation and set themselves free from the order-stricken tensions of machine life.

Likewise, in the city, our inner software hastily starts processing the individuals' clothes and clothing styles (making distinctions, comparison, evaluation, and the like). For instance, our software considers preset-color criteria as an indicator for the assessment of one's clothing colors and taste (i.e. cold color, warm color, color combination ratio along with their compatibility, etc), and accordingly draws conclusions such as the individual's good- or bad-taste in choosing clothing colors.

In cases where clothing colors do not conform to the person's inner preprogrammed software, they unconsciously become irritated. A villager's worldview, as a result of his intimate contact and connection with nature, is not programmed based on such criteria; therefore, they are not disturbed when they see different [non-matching] colors used beside one another. They have learnt well from nature that any color can be used beside any other color, and that, nature's coloring is extremely beautiful although it lacks any specific criteria (pattern or combination).

People living in the countryside are more adjusted with nature. The closer we become to nature, the more distant will our minds be from orderly arrangements, symmetries, color harmonies, and the like, and the more freely will it act. The fabrics of a rural lady's clothing widely differ from that of an urban lady. A great variety of colors are viewed in the rustic clothing and diverse [non-matching] colors are placed next to each other that are a unique beauty of the village life.

Likewise is a rural mind that functions freely, in accordance with nature and independent of urban orders and logical constraints. As a result, such disorderliness not only creates no tension or stress on the individual but they actually bring him pleasure. Conversely, in the city, due to our mental programs that are captive in the order framework, such color matching gives us an unpleasant feeling. In fact, city-dwellers have lost their conformity with nature.

Take the body colors of the fish, for example, that are composed of various weird and bizarre colors to which the human eye is often unaccustomed. If the human being was to design the fishes' bodies he would never apply such color combination; Whereas, the person accustomed to nature is familiar with this color matching and their life is even inspired by it.

The more we study, the better we conclude that correcting one's worldview and accepting the coexistence of *Order and Disorder* is more natural and ensures better health. To complete this study an essential question needs to be answered: is order for life, or life for order? Does health serve orderliness or does order serve health? And how far can one go for maintaining order?

Obviously the immediate reply that springs to mind is that: order is to support living and it should serve human health. Yet, many housewives put their cardiac health at risk as they insist on creating an order that is beyond their capabilities. In other words, they simply sacrifice their well-being for keeping such [down to the last detail] order which is actually unreachable. Keeping order is appropriate to the extent that it does not damage the human health. This limit is the acceptable degree for maintaining orderliness.

It is worth mentioning that there are at least two types of order maintenance:

(1) Implementation of civic and public order within a legal framework and based on civic and social life requirements, such as traffic rules and the like.

(2) Enforcing order within personal and family living environment.

Here we discuss the latter case and its relation to well-being. The individuals are to reach a status in which disorderliness cannot threaten their health or expose them to irretrievable losses. This does not imply that they must deliberately cause disorderliness or wish for it. On the contrary, it is to say that although individuals should establish order to the best of their ability, in case of deficiency, they should neither be obsessive about it nor become unhealthy. And it should have no negative effect whatsoever on them.

The permitted limit for keeping order is *relative*. For instance someone might be able to clean up his/her place twice or three times a day, while another person can do so only once a week or once a month. Which one is more appropriate? And, to what point should one maintain order? The reply is already mentioned: maintaining order is necessary to the extent that our strength allows and one should never waste their health on it.

The Relationship Between Order and Disorder Law And Abnormal Behaviors

At times, we witness incidents in the society that justifying the motivations behind them seems difficult. Take for instance: damaging telephone boxes, bus seats, train windows, and the like. Evidence shows that those who carry out such actions take pleasure in doing so. They rarely seem to quit such behavior and might even keep this habit for a lifetime. Moreover, there are individuals from wealthy and respectable families who -without any financial needs- repeatedly commit theft. A handful of analyses exist regarding such abnormal behaviors. Psychologists, sociologists, and others each try to get to the root of the problem their own way.

A baby's world is in accordance with the universe's frameworks and is programmed based on the law of Order and Disorder. For example, a kid who deeply aspires to possess a toy and then finally gets hold of it through great persistence. He plays with it for a while and does not allow anyone else to even touch it. Nevertheless, after a while he starts to break it down into pieces on purpose. In fact, a baby's mentality is in concordance to [the principles of] 'Construction and Deconstruction', and 'Order and Disorder'.

However, most parents, just for their own ease, desire their children to only utilize one single half of their existing software-based program and to merely apply 'order' in all aspects of their lives. The world-viewing software of both parents and teachers are set up based on order and logic; therefore, they insist that their kids act likewise and based on the same world-viewing system from infanthood. Consequently, they suggest ration, order and logic to their kids. Later on, they even boast about their very rational and neat children.

The core basis of all the efforts of parents and educational systems is to enforce more and more orderliness on kids, or as they put it, to educate kids with orderliness. But this way, one part of the child's existing software becomes futile. In fact, this [enforced] program contradicts the child's normal software and as soon as he is less controlled (usually during adolescence), this contradiction manifests itself. The conflicts between these two programs results in rebellion of the youth against logic and order (discipline). A rebellion which is subconscious and which automatically gives the individual pleasure whenever disrupting orderliness.

When such individuals see a clean and well-ordered telephone box, they unconsciously and inadvertently try to spoil its order by damaging it, and they enjoy doing so. Whatever symbolizes order [or pattern] unknowingly annoys them and forces them to act destructively. For instance, the moving of a train that is a symbol of orderliness disturbs them indirectly, and they would go into raptures if they could somehow break this order even by throwing a stone at the moving train. So, they do so, and it brings them absolute delight without knowing why. Generally, after imposing logic and order on children, an 'order-stricken' and 'logic-stricken' complication is shaped in their subconscious as a result of which they unknowingly challenge orderliness and whatever symbolizes it.

In more developed societies that enforce more discipline, we witness more serious incidents and disruptive behaviors when the order-stricken and logic-stricken phase exposes itself. For instance, in the West (with a more advanced technology and systematic order) every so often we hear the news of an armed teenager entering a school and opening fire on the school kids. In some people, the uprising against order is demonstrated through a reversed mechanism, i.e. they act opposite and contrary to what they are told. In very large families where individuals are engaged in a type of dictatorships, such rebellion is revealed in a different manner.

Another type of rebellion against order and logic is the sexual orientation response in which the person grimaces at reason, logic and order, and unconsciously reacts against normal sexual orientation. The human being's inner software is programmed based on attraction to the opposite sex (heterosexuality); however, as a result of this rebellion it is changed to attraction to the same sex (homosexuality). For the reason that this opposes part of the logic that governs human behavior, it unconsciously satisfies the individual and they will enjoy such tendency. The more man is forced into logic and order, the more will homosexual tendencies and the like increase. This is one of the current problems of the world, and the more human beings move towards machine life and absolute order and logic, the more will they face such issues.

Some homosexuals never ask themselves why they have such a tendency; while others who are aware of their issue, seek the underlying cause and its solution. If the condition is permanent and enduring, one of the below reasons plays a role in it:

(1) Software-based factor

(2) Being programmed based on the law of Order and Disorder (an

unconscious rebellion against discipline and logic)

(3) The initial programming of the unconscious software in childhood

(4) Being contaminated with 'non-organic viruses'[5]

(5) Others

The software-based factor is defined as changes in the individual's normal software-based programs of the unconscious as a result of events, and their replacement with new programs which accordingly form such tendencies. For instance, when a young girl is repeatedly told that "she is so much like her father", in her subconscious software -that is extremely programmable during infancy and childhood- it is written that she is like her farther. This is then put next to the other [pre-entered] information of [the unconscious] software telling her that 'her father is a man'. After a while, these two statements are processed and combined in the individual's subconscious, and several years later and in adolescence, she considers herself a man from the inside and not a woman. She is therefore attracted to her same sex and not to the opposite one. At the same time, she is unaware how she got into such a situation and how this program was created. In other words, homosexuality, that is often considered to be a sexual perversion by the public, has happened unconsciously.

Similarly, some might dress up their young boy as a girl just for the

---

5- One of the most indispensable theories in Psymentology is the 'non-organic viruses theory'. According to this theory, the human being is encountered with viruses that could affect his mind, body and psyche; infiltrate in man's diverse existing constituents and data files, having them contaminated with parasites and derangements. When such parasites occupy the mind data files, they consequently bring about all kinds of hallucinations, abnormal behaviors and unusual drives. In Psymentology there is a specific approach towards these types of disorders and the treatment for such cases lies within a special branch of treatment called 'defensive emission' or 'psymento-therapy' (For details please refer to Non-organic Beings, M.A. Taheri).

fun of it, and put on make-up for him or ask him to act like girls. Or parents, who wished to have a daughter, might pick a girl's name for their son and treat him like a girl [these examples vary from culture to culture]. After a while the child's unconscious software is likely to be convinced that 'he is a girl'. Thus, in adolescence, he might show attraction to his own sex, a tendency that others consider as a homosexual inclination, but he himself views as normal.

In both cases, the first factor that is the entrance of incorrect programs into the individual's unconscious software has caused such conditions. Thus, the person is a '*software-based victim*'. As discussed, the second factor (rebellion against *Order and Disorder*) is also a major cause of homosexuality in which the person is again considered a victim.

With a closer look at the above explanation, it can be stated that so far the human beings' unawareness of the laws and principles of the universe has caused him more damage than imagined. For instance, the damages caused by neglecting the *Order and Disorder law* (that include various types of rebellion -a few of which were mentioned above-, and even sadism, masochism, and the like) expand day by day. On the contrary, recognizing the application of such laws and their true place will bring the human being a healthier life.

3. The Law of Birth and Death

What gives the material world meaning and directs its motion is the *law of birth and death*. This is one of the general, major and universal laws that govern the material world and all its constituents. For instance, a phenomenon such as the big bang is [in fact] *birth and death* at the level of the whole ecosystem; a part of the material world. Furthermore, phenomena such as the black hole and supernovas are a result of *birth and death* of its constituents. They are indications of this law that make the material world move.

يكسان سازى شود

The presence of each constituent of the universe starts with a *birth* and moves towards a *death*, to be reborn in another state. To provide further explanation we can discuss the sun. The sun -like other constituents of the universe- experiences the stages of birth, life and death and is currently in its middle age.

The sun was born in the form of a rich source of hydrogen, concurrent with the formation of the solar system. Since then, it started to burn and to consume its energy reserves. In this process, when two atoms of hydrogen are combined, one atom of helium is created, and because the atomic mass density of helium is less than that of the two atoms of hydrogen together, a mass shortage happens which, according to Einstein's formula, is then converted into energy. Considering the trend in which the sun is consuming its stored hydrogen to generate energy, this storage will eventually reach an end. Thereafter, helium will start to burn which itself will be the beginning of the formation of heavier elements on the surface of this gigantic celestial mass.

Accordingly, the surface gravity of the sun will increase. The sun will then start to crumple up until it is shrunk to the size of a football. In this state, its surface gravity shall increase noticeably so that even light cannot escape from it. The time has finally arrived for the sun to die. The sun turns into a black hole which continuously increases in density until it reaches the critical density level, and an explosion occurs that is indeed another *birth*. As a result, the supernova born from the heart of this explosion once more generates the same process at the heart of the material world in a different form.

Similar processes of *birth and death* are experienced by infinite universal constituents all across the vast universe and there is no running from it. After the death of stars such as the sun and the formation of black holes, sets such as the planet Earth and its moons are sucked into them. Hence, they approach their death.

The human being -as an inseparable constituent of the universe- is also subject to the law of *birth and death,* and he has no possibility whatsoever to escape from it. Death is the definite manifestation of God's grace which calls on everyone [and everything] without exception. It embraces all constituents of the universe including humans in a particular way. Without death, human beings would become trapped in the eternal need of earthly life and they would be forced to satisfy necessities such as food and clothing, accommodation, and the like for thousands and thousands of years. In fact, death is part of an intelligent plan which, on the one hand, puts an end to human's needs and, on the other hand, is the transforming factor (from one state to another) that prevents them from living a stagnant and static life.

This extremely intelligent plan rescues the human being from the state of highest conflict and does not allow them to remain in need and deep darkness for all eternity. Death is the determining factor as to human being's return to Him.

No factor other than death can guide us towards Him step by step. However, considering the human being's feeble ability to recognize, understand and perceive this divine plan, the phenomenon of death has become compulsory and movement towards Him inherent. Otherwise, the never-ending excuses of the majority of people would prevent movement towards Him. In other words, due to the lack of knowledge about this divine path (that is the *ilayhe-rajeoon* path) and not recognizing one's true benefit, the human beings would still prefer to stay in this world of needs. Therefore, God's grace has been once more conferred on mankind in this case, by making everyone experience death without exception and calling them towards Himself.

Wherever ye may be, death will overtake you, even though ye were in lofty towers.

-Quran; Sura An-nisa, Verse 78

In the world of mysticism, one of the greatest love affairs is the love affair with death. There is no mystic who has not experienced such love and who has not demonstrated enthusiasm for meeting God and joining Him.

Why be afraid of death when it approaches?
Isn't it a path towards Thee that I well know?
Death is neither a garden nor a park
it is a way to the abode of the Beloved
So, why should I mourn my death?
When He is the one who makes it happen, I well wish for it!
If one views the truth behind it
death is not seen as a death anymore, but a mere relocation
from a small cottage to a house
and from a house to a royal feast.
Since this sleep guides me to Thy feast
I will utterly accept it
As long as this joy and enthusiasm exists
I will joyfully sleep to awake once more.

-Nezami Ganjavi

A mystic is not attached to life. He eagerly awaits the divine royal feast that is beyond this transient world, and his being is entirely filled with the burning desire for such presence. Thus, the mystic awaits the moment in which he surrenders his soul to God and enters His feast.

My soul that is entrusted to me by the Beloved

I will surrender it back to Him, as soon as we meet.

-Hafez

The mystic does not have a sense of belonging to this earthly world. He considers a preeminent position for his existence which can only be reclaimed through death.

I am a bird from the garden of heaven
I am not from the earthly world
They have made me a bodily cage only for a few days

-Molana Rumi

He well knows that his true life begins when he is freed from this life of complete need.

I am well aware that my life is my death
I become eternal only once freed from this life

-Molana Rumi

The mystic ceaselessly counts down the seconds to become a stage closer to Him. He knows very well that he nears Him through death. Furthermore, as a result of this closeness, the individual's needs also decrease until he finally finds himself in the arm of his Rab, and such neediness comes to an end.

Oh! How I wish for the day in which I shall fly to the side of my Beloved
To flutter freely around Him
-Molana Rumi

Of course, the enthusiasm for death does not indicate that one should overlook the precious opportunity of life. And quite the opposite, it is necessary to increase this opportunity as much as possible. The human being cannot violate the laws governing the universe that include the law of *death*; however, they can intelligently use these laws to their own benefits.

As mentioned in the book '*Human from Another Outlook*', the natural longevity of humans has a coefficient in which the individual plays a crucial role. In an attempt to get the maximum benefit and result from this stage of the movement within the *ilayhe-rajeoon* path, the individual can increase this longevity. Exactly like a student who, at the last minute of his exam, tries to make the ultimate use of the remaining short time to answer at least one more question, an aware individual also endeavors to get the maximum benefit from his presence in this stage. Thus, he seeks a longer life.

For each of us to understand as to whether we are living life compliant with the divine plan or we are playing a role in the satanic plan, through a moment's reflection and evaluation, we can find an answer to the question: 'Am I afraid of death or not?'. A positive answer manifests that we are following Satan's plan. However, if without any feelings of depression and [sense of] escape from life the answer is 'No', it indicates that we are living in accordance with the divine plan.

Since opposing the laws of the [symbolic] *book of the universe* (the book of apparent divine signs) inevitably causes the human beings to suffer serious loss and harm, withstanding and obstinacy against the *law of death* can also cause psycheal and mental imbalances, and consequently lead to physical disorders. In other words, when we do not accept this law that is one of the most indisputable laws of the universe and we resist it, we will certainly suffer '*the fear of death*' which is one of the major reasons that individuals become affected by various mental, psycheal and physical illnesses. In such cases, similar to all other mentosomatic disorders that originate from [incorrect] worldview, the *mind*, *psyche* and physical body become involved respectively.

4. The Law of Change

The *law of change* is another law regulating the universe that acts similar to the *law of birth and death*. What differentiates them is that the *law of birth and death* has an effect in the long term while the *law of change* is instant. This law covers both the whole material world and its constituents at any given moment. That is to say, everything is subject to instant change. Therefore, none of the constituents of the universe are as they were a second ago and they are all constantly changing from one state and condition to another.

> *Nothing is stable and lasting*
> *Everything is constantly changing and evolving*

> *-Molana Rumi*

The universal *law of change* causes instant change from one state to another and the movement towards the very milestone of *birth and death*. It is the change and transformation that makes everything distinctly different from its previous state. The *law of change* leads everything towards this milestone.

This law does not exclusively cover objects and is the cause of many of the incidents that the human being deals with. Through this law, the individuals' adaptability to change and their preparedness to face what appears to be negative and unpleasant changes can be studied, and it can be evaluated whether or not the individual is ready to accept such inevitable changes.

There is no escape whatsoever from the *law of change*. This law plows the farm of the universe so that the *birth and death* of the tree of life take place in it. Without becoming aware of this law and accepting it, we will suffer severe mental, psycheal and physical trauma in [certain] conditions that we consider the changes to be unpleasant, and we will incur the secondary losses and harms of such rejection. Changes such as premature aging, depression, losing one's teeth, hair, and the like are due to the individuals' rejection of change. Nevertheless, by becoming aware of this law and accepting and applying it, we will definitely remain immune to such disorders in many cases.

5. The Law of Uniqueness and Unrepeatability

No two moments in time and no two particles are the same in the universe, and no event is repeated twice. In other words; 'A man will never swim in the same river twice.'

We acquire knowledge about atoms, crystals, their essence and different properties through science; however, most of us do not know that no two atoms of an element are identical and that no two similar crystals exist. For instance, although all hydrogen atoms function in the same way, no two identical atoms of hydrogen have ever existed since the beginning of creation and will never exist. Each atom is a micro world [by itself] with a greatness that conforms to that of the material world.

Microcosmos = Macrocosmos

The world of an atom = The universe

However, the number of motions, orbital, particles, anti-particles and infinite constituents of each atom testify that there is no possibility of two micro worlds (of two atoms) to be simultaneously identical.

In addition to the uniqueness of every single particle of the universe, all the Omnipotent's creations, similar to an unrepeatable and unique work of art, are also unique in their own way. Akin to an artist who paints the same painting of a landscape twice, despite their apparently striking resemblance, the two paintings are not identical. God's design in every single constituent of the universe is an unrepeatable masterpiece and none of His two creations are alike.

In regard to the human being who consists of infinite constituents (trillions of cells, molecules, infinite atoms and many other non-physical bodies) and is considered as a vast universe, this unrepeatability is [completely] obvious. Each human being has always been, is, and will always be only one of its kind. Even identical twins or cloned humans are not identical, and despite their very similar appearance they are different, even from the inside.

Each human being is a divine masterpiece, and one of the reasons behind the disapprobation of suicide is the very same point. Because, by committing suicide, a masterpiece and an unrepeatable work of art that can never be replaced is wiped out from the scene of life. Lack of attention to this law causes the human being's value not to be taken into account as it ought to, and the individual will have a superficial viewpoint about the universe. Through recognizing the *law of uniqueness and unrepeatability,* each and every particle of the universe is viewed with respect, because the existence of everything is the work of art and unrepeatable masterpiece of the Creator which will never be replaced and will remain to be one of a kind.

In general, an individual who is in the darkened night of unawareness does not know their value and place. Thus, they might pursue a goal other than attaining one's [true] status (as a divine unique manifestation) and become heedless of their duty and deviate from it. In fact, human beings have to find their value as the divine manifestation. In this case, they will view everything from a different perspective, and the status and value of each constituent of the universe will be revealed to them in such a way that they see nothing but God in them.

Wherever you might turn, there is the Image of God.
- Quran; Sura Baqarah, Verse 115

Human will reach a status in which he sees nothing but God
Look how a supreme status one can reach.

- Saadi

Each of God's creations has been created in its ultimate perfection (*Kamal*) and no creation has been designed incomplete. Now, if a person who believes in God denies *the law of uniqueness and unrepeatability* they should be asked;

Could God have possibly created something incomplete?

Could God have possibly made a mistake in creation of something?

And, could God have possibly wanted to fix His previous mistake by recreating the same thing?

6. Perihelion and Aphelion Law (Fountain Law)

Astronomical objects follow an elliptical orbit, and depending on their axis of movement which is located at one of the ellipse's focal points, they are at aphelion or perihelion[6]. In other words, celestial bodies demonstrate the *law of summit and trough* in the material world, which can also be called the *law of distance and closeness* or the *law of separation and reunification.*

Each unification is the beginning of a separation, and each separation, the beginning of unification. Without separation, unification is meaningless, as is unification without separation. Everything that

---

6- The words "aphelion" and "perihelion" come from the Greek language. In Greek, "helios" mean Sun, "peri" means near, and "apo" means away from.

approaches (including difficulties and conveniences [of life], the good and bad times, and so on) will eventually move away. Conversely, what is currently distant will eventually approach. In addition, when anything (including emotions, desires, social positions and the like) reach their summit, they will eventually reach their trough (*fountain law*).

> *Do not dream of a union without any separation*
> *Since a state of drunkenness comes with its aftereffects.*

-Saadi

However, the human beings yearn to change this law of the universe as per their desire, and they demand [nothing but] unification and want to be in constant union with what they are attached to. For example, if the individual is in the path of progress, he desires this ascent to last forever. Nevertheless, based on this law, everything that ascends will definitely descend one day.

Many people who are financially successful are not prepared to lose it. They believe that things will always remain the same. Thus, during a sudden descent and fall, they suffer from mental, psycheal and physical difficulties because they had not anticipated it and were not prepared for accepting the new situation.

Many people become ill due to the lack of awareness about the *law of separation and unification*. They think that their spouse, children and others will always remain by their side; however, their separation might be inevitable due to [unforeseen] circumstances. Thus, we encounter many difficulties in case of discordance with the laws of the universe.

With a look back into history, we see that the ups and downs of history all occurred based on this law. Many kings, sultans and emperors who were once at the summit of their power and could never have imagined the fall of their reign, suddenly found themselves in the 'trough' point.

A big mistake that has constantly been repeated throughout history is unawareness of the *law of perihelion and aphelion*.

This law strengthens human beings' *'power to lose'*. Since the ultimate power that mankind can achieve is the power to lose, it is said that the *law of summit and trough* teaches human beings the lesson to achieve this highest strength. So that, at the time of descent and loss, the individual is capable of withstanding the situation with full strength and will not suffer various mental, psycheal and physical damages. Furthermore, this law gives hope to those who are in extreme difficulty and hopelessness, because it promises that 'the dark night ends with daylight' and that 'with every difficulty there is surely ease.'[7]

In the world of mysticism, *perihelion and aphelion* is equivalent to separation from and union with the Beloved (God). However, the transformation achieved on the path of Kamal brings the individual such stability that *distance and closeness* [from God] lose their meanings.

> *What is the importance of being far from or close to the Beloved?*
> *One should seek nothing but His consent*
> *Otherwise it would be a shame to ask anything from Him other than His own self.*
> *-Hafez*

In this state, the governing law is the law of the *'[burning] candle and the butterfly'*, and similar to a butterfly only flying to [the fire of] the candle, the individual spins on the axis of God alone. The individual's *Axis of Existence*[8] conforms to this oneness-viewing and unity-seeking. In such a state, [the saying that] 'There is no axis and no power but in God' is institutionalized in the person's existence. In fact, his *Axis of*

7- Quran; Sura Al-inshirah, Verse 6
8- Please refer to foot note number 5, chapter 2.

Existence is that very axis of the Beloved (God); thus, he is no more concerned about being in separation or union. For him revolving around a single axis has become a basic principle, and he desires nothing else.

> *One desires pain, another healing*
> *One desires union, another separation*
> *From pain, healing, union and separation*
> *I desire what my Beloved desires*
> *-Baba Taher*

7. Dynamic in Static Law

When we look at the sky, we see all the stars and celestial objects in complete peace and stillness (static), and since we do not notice their movement we assume that they lack a starting point and a destination, and that they have all reached their destination and are not moving towards another one. It appears as if their existence and presence are merely important, and that the purpose behind their creation is summarized in their 'being'. The deep peace that governs their presence gives the impression that they have had no beginning and will have no end. Nevertheless, every single constituent of the universe is continuously rendered by a gentle movement.

> *Everything is in a move and yet constantly still*
> *As if it has no beginning and no end*
>
> *-Shabestari*

All constituents of the universe are announcing their presence in this divine manifestation whilst for them '*moving ahead*' is a sign of '*being*'. Their message of peace is the ultimate purpose of their presence in a space wherein 'reaching' has no significance and is nothing more than a pretext.

Each phenomenon in the universe carries a message for the human being. The message that is received from the gentle and endless motion of celestial objects and other constituents of the universe is the lesson of living in the present moment. It teaches the hasty human being that everything flows in the very second. Thus, if we know how to benefit from each given moment, it could be our *immediate paradise*.

Furthermore, with a closer look at the constituents of the universe, contrary to their static appearance, we encounter extraordinary acceleration and speed in the heart of each constituent. In other words, the universe is static in its reality and appearance, and is dynamic in its truth and essence. But, the human being's behavior does not conform to this characteristic of the *book of the universe* (which is the model that guides the human being). Apparently, humans are so on the move and in search of something that it seems they want to move the world. However, in truth, they are not really doing anything positive and noticeable. They are indeed stagnant in the essence of their movement.

It is necessary for the human being to be symphasic with the universe. They should conform to its patterns because wherever they lack the essential conformity, it definitely causes problems. One of the consequences of the modern life is the hastiness feature, and due to its incompliance with the *dynamic in static law*, not only do time and the heaven stand against human being, they also make humans encounter *God's rage* in other forms.

God's rage is lawful. It happens when we do not observe the universe's natural laws and behave inappropriately towards them. In truth, *God's rage* is the natural punishment which happens within the framework of divine laws, and it is imposed on the human that stands against the universe. For instance, not making optimized use of the atmosphere's oxygen leads to the melting of the polar ice caps during a certain process which subsequently launches a tremendous storm such as the *flood of Noah*. This is considered *God's rage* that is [in fact] caused by human's mistakes. In other words, *God's rage* is the lawful reflection and the outcome of human's negative deeds.

The hastiness which has greatly entrapped today's man, throws them off their mental and psycheal balance and eventually leads to physical disorders. Insomnia, stress, dyspepsia and many other disorders are among such irretrievable complications.

8. Interaction Law

Each constituent of the universe influences all the other constituents and is affected by them. The same reality is true of the human being. We humans have an effect on one another and on the entire constituents of the material world, and are mutually influenced by them.

No particle or creature is exception to the *interaction law*. The universe is itself a Unified Body with a precise relationship between all its constituents. The infinite constituents of the human existence also interact with one another as one [single] world. For instance, all the cells of the human body are in connection with one another, and in the case of positive interaction, the system will show its best efficiency. However, once a cell acts outside its natural process, hundred trillions of other cells will become endangered. It is therefore not applicable to say that the value and effect of a single cell can be completely ignored in comparison with the other hundred trillions of cells. If a cell develops cancer, other cells are exposed to the danger of metastasis, and a cell's abnormal proliferation will be spread to other cells.

Each human being is similar to a cell in an enormous body. In this body -that is formed by the collection of [all] human beings- each individual has to help others grow to subsequently benefit from the interaction of this positive growth. In a society, the decline of even one individual causes the whole society to undergo the loss of that fall. One of the compensations that the society pays for individual's fall is losing its public security. In societies with a higher public culture the rate of crime is less and such a society will be subject to less damage.

The children of humanity are each others' limbs
that shares an origin in their creation
when one limb is in pain
the other limbs cannot remain easy
-Sa'adi

According to the *interaction law*; If an individual wants to grow, they have to promote the growth of others (the theory of *collective growth* and *public salvation*). If an individual prevents the growth of others by any means, pulls them down for his own ascent, and ruins their cultural health, he will ultimately incur loss himself; causing him to fall. In addition, their children, grandchildren, and generally the next generation and heirs will undergo the loss sustained by these mistakes just as we are currently paying the price for the mistakes and negligence of our previous generations.

9. Action and Reaction Law

In the material world each action has a reaction. This law, called the *action and reaction law,* is one of the laws of the world of conflict that also applies to human beings, because behind each human action and thought there lays a reaction delivering the result of that thought or action.

With an observant eye
The answers to all actions are observable in every single second

If you are aware, be careful of
What you create with your each and every act
-Molana Rumi

The universe is like a mountain where each sound is accompanied by an echo (returning to its origin). It can also be resembled to a farm. If the individual plants barley in it, he reaps barley, and if wheat is planted, the harvest is wheat. Thus, we should expect the answer to our deeds, behaviors and thoughts every moment.

Although one's shadow may grow on the wall
It will finally get back to him
This world is a mountain and our acts echoes
The sound of echoes will return back to us

-Molana Rumi

No human deed lacks the subsequent noticeable or unnoticeable reaction. However, part of these reactions return instantaneously '*...and God is quick in account*'[9]. For instance, when we hate or feel agitation and are in a state of worry, the brain immediately orders the secretion of poisonous chemicals. Thereafter, the body is poisoned and its negative consequences which involve different disorders appear.

The market of punishment of deeds is so active that
with an open eye, every day is the Judgment Day.
-Sa'adi

Another part of the consequences of human behaviors have long-term effects on the world. It happens in a wavelike form and with a time delay. For example, a lady or a gentleman leaves the house in the morning to go to work. On their way to work they might have a verbal argument

---

9- Quran; Sura Al-baqara, Verse 202

with another person and then the second person makes another person angry in another way. This wave continues spreading sequentially, so that, when the same lady or gentlemen returns home at night, they receive the intangible effect of the very same wave [this time] from their family members, neighbors, relatives, friends, and the like. The continuation of this wave even strikes the next generation, and owing to the transferred effects, their posterity has to additionally pay for this yet very little anger.

10. Continuity Law

There is continuity among the constituents of any collection of the universe. For the same reason, we witness time continuity and place continuity (continuity in matter and energy).

Law of Matter and Energy Continuity:

Not only are matter and energy in universal continuity with each other, but also the place of each particle is determined within the universe by its continuity with other particles of the universe, in such a way that eliminating any constituent will disturb this system.

> *If you take one single particle out of its place*
> *The whole existence will be disturbed.*
> *-Shabestari*

Law of Time Continuity:

The state of each particle in the present time depends on its past, and its future state is the product of its current position. In addition, the particle's appearance also varies depending on time. If time was to be eliminated, particles would take a completely different form than what we currently observe. This is because the infinite numbers of [a particle's] forms which belong to different times, will be superimposed onto each other and will all be seen as one. In other words, each object has infinite shapes and forms by itself that have become distinct based on time, and if superimposed onto each other, their form and appearance completely alters.

The human eye views only one frame of the object (the shape that is related to a particular instant). Therefore, in case of eliminating time, the individual will have an image of the whole universe in front of him where everything is observed with its origin. Thus, we will reach the *tree of life* or the *tree of the universe* in which all creations have a common root. This tree is in fact the image of the universe's Unified Body [viewed] from a standpoint beyond [the dimension of] time.

Each particle is both the product of the existence of its previous second, and the origin for its own existence in the coming second. It is at the same time in continuity with other particles. The human being, as a member of the universe, cannot sever themselves from connection with time and place because their existence is the result of a process undergone throughout history. That is to say, the modern man is not separated from the primitive man, and he has reached his current situation through a long process.

Mankind (the collection of the human beings throughout history), has moved through different stages within his movement which have resulted in his intellectual and inner maturity. Very similar to the stages of the human life from conception to birth and death, mankind is also going through different stages that include: conception, embryo, infancy, childhood, adolescence, youth, middle age, and old age. At each stage he shows the same features that characterize that stage of human life. For instance, identical to an infant who lacks wisdom and the ability to differentiate and only acts based on instinct, mankind -in his infancy- also lacked wisdom as it is known today. He led an animal like life and it took him a very long time to pass this stage.

The childhood stage coincides with the activation of wisdom. In this stage, the child eventually recognizes his surroundings and discovers himself. However, the child is not yet familiar with the world of love. Mankind, in his childhood stage, also reached the early stages of wisdom and succeeded in building, discovering and using tools, and providing clothing, food, housing, and the like in order to maintain life. In this way, mankind stepped into the '*wisdom era*' wherein there is certainly no familiarity with love and its consequences yet.

For instance, in the '*wisdom era*' or mankind's childhood, the taste for poetry did not manifest. Exactly like a child, they only attempted to discover their surrounding, declared their intentions and fulfilled their basic life necessities.

In the same way that the signs of the individual's taste are manifested in adolescence, and it is during this stage that the individual becomes familiar with love and demonstrates the effects of his talents, mankind also gained the set of experiences related to the world of love in his teenage years. However, without being analyzed, the consequences of these experiences remained raw and blind in this stage. And so, mankind did not realize their purpose.

In his youth, mankind was able to completely perceive love and its consequences, and the greatest part of literary, romantic and inspirational works emerged in this romantic era.

At present, mankind is in his middle age. He has the ability to reach a conclusion about love and have a more mature look at it. Thereafter, his old age arrives. In this stage mankind writes a thesis which wraps up his historical effort and his experiences of wisdom and love, and the general plan of creation will be revealed.

According to scientific reports, the human body's cells change every eight years. Meaning that each eight years, the human body transforms into a whole new body and the old cells are replaced with the new ones. However, with the change of the physical body, the individual's identity is preserved in continuity with his present and past. This means that his childhood is not lost. Therefore, mankind's previous generation (even the Neanderthal humans) is considered a part of his existence, and we are all in continuity with each other and are not separated. The unity of Adam's body is discovered when this issue is observed from different angles.

Neglecting the *continuity law* results in a way of thinking that creates multiplicity and disturbance of the *mind*, *psyche* and so on. Consequently, the body will not remain immune from the resultant harm.

11. Connectedness Law

In the universe, every constituent has meaning and identity in relation to other constituents, and the existence of each individual is meaningful with the existence of other individuals. Suppose that a person lives on an island all by himself. In this case, would it matter to have a name? If the individual was assured that no one is or will be present to communicate with them or their artwork, would they even bother to draw figures or write letters as a means of conveying their intention? Would they create an artwork and the like?

The answer to such questions is 'No'! A painter attempts to paint in order to communicate indirectly with other humans. In fact, art comes to life when other people exist and when there is the possibility to interact with others.

The very first stage of *art* is when humans interact with one another directly, and the highest level of art is keeping this relationship along the axis of affection and unity. In such an elevated relation, humans even circumvent intermediary factors such as poetry, painting, music and the like, and their art would be to create an inner attraction that leads to unity and closeness between them. Accordingly, repellency is the ultimate disgrace and the true lack of art.

In general, the universe has been designed based on *presentation* and everything in it makes sense through presentation. This is also what gives value to the communication between humans. It shows the manner in which the individual relates to others, the way they evaluate this connection and the results they attain from it. In fact, the individual's motivation and the way they relate [to others] indicate what they are presenting to the universe.

In summary, no human being carries a meaning per se and the existence of each human being is meaningful in relation to the existence of others and as a result of communicating with them. All humans are the [various] manifestations of 'one single self' (Adam), and in order to take on a meaning or to give meaning to others, they need to communicate with one another and with the universe.

In this *world of multiplicity* many individuals might not be able to tolerate other individuals. They think that if they were all alone on the planet Earth and if no one else existed, they would be more peaceful and would have a better life. They are indeed not aware that if this was the case, they could never be defined and would never be able to discover themselves.

We can compare all the humans throughout history to the cells of one body. Therefore, all their actions and thoughts are interconnected with one another, and even if one person does not think or behave properly, mankind altogether suffers the loss and harm of that thought and performance. For this reason, the future generations continuously experience the effects of wrong- or right- records of their previous generations' functions.

12. Conflict Law

One of the main laws of the material world is the law of conflict which establishes the framework of this world. Human's knowledge and whatever they comprehend are furthermore a result of the existence of conflict. When a truth is not subject to conflict, the human being is definitely unable to perceive it. For instance, we are not able to know the nature of God and to define it.

> *The manifestation of any subject is due to their opposites*
> *Except God that is the all incomparable and unique one.*
> *Since His nature is unique*
> *I do not know how you could possibly become to know Him?*
> *-Shabestari*

Conflicting issues are discoverable and recordable only, and whatever is hidden to the human eye has the capability to manifest itself only if it is conflicting.

> *All that is hidden can be revealed through their opposites*
> *Since God has no opposite, He is concealed.*

> *-Molana Rumi*

In general, individuals deal with a constant stream of conflicts all throughout their lives and the existence of conflicts is the very factor for their growth. The Creator has created human beings inside a world based on conflicts, providing them a basis for reaching transcendence. Without the existence of such basis, Adam's (mankind) potential ability could not develop into actual ability, and he would stagnate.

> *God created suffering and sorrow,*
> *So that happiness manifests through its opposite*
> *The hidden, are manifested through their opposites*
> *God remains hidden as he lacks opposite*
> *At first light appeared and then the colors*

Everything is distinguished by its opposite, like black and white
So you know light by anti-light
Opposites manifest each other in your heart

-*Molana Rumi*

Since life is itself formed based on *birth and death*, it is the product of the existence of conflict. Any conflicting happening or phenomenon is exposed to destruction and perdition, and anything that breaks itself free from conflict can escape destruction and attain immortality. In other words, conflict is the cause of tiredness and atrophy, and the lack of conflict is the reason for immortality.

This world lives by the war of the opposites
Peace between the opposites is eternal life.

-*Molana Rumi*

Incompatibility of the individuals' worldview with the *conflict law* and the fact that everything gains its meaning through the manifestation of its opposite cause conflict between the human being and God's plan of creation. No one can eradicate the *conflict law* which is a divine law. Without conflict, the universe would possess a completely different form and relations, but now that it is established based on conflicts, we can artistically control the inner manifestation of its factors, and thus reach a valuable result through this control. Not accepting the *conflict law* increases one's inner conflicts with all the pillars of the universe, and it leads to the individual's stress, poison and the illnesses caused by it.

13. Predestination Law

All constituents of the universe are ruled by the *predestination law* and no constituent has a way to escape from it. The predestinated movement of the universe which is the '*ilayhe-rajeoon*' movement is also called the '*inherent movement*'. According to the '*inherent movement*', everything certainly returns back to God, and no constituent has the possibility of escaping from this movement. The predestinated or inherent movement can be compared to the movement of a train on a railroad. It has departed from a certain starting point and it reaches a destination after passing through certain routes. But then again, its passengers can move inside the passenger cars voluntarily and they are free to carry out different activities. As a conclusion, '*predestination*' and '*free will*' rule the human being's overall movement.

One of the worldview problems is the lack of knowledge, understanding, and perception of the '*predestination law*'. In other words, all the laws of the universe are a manifestation of the divine predestination that in turn gives meaning to human's free will. The human being raises the question about why we have to move in a certain [predefined] direction (questioning predestination in the inherent movement). This question is raised due to our unawareness of the role of the human being and the importance of this role which determines the quality and manner of the [inherent] movement path. As a consequence, not having a correct worldview regarding the *predestination law* additionally causes conflict with God, with the universe, one's self and with others. Consequently, it is one of the factors that cause illness in the human beings.

14. Weed Law

A farmer endures considerable difficulties until the desired crop grows. At the same time, a weed grows faster than the main crop without any need for cultivation or any type of handling and attention. The weed is stronger than the crop and it tolerates the cold, heat, dehydration and the like better than the actual crop. Even though the farmer has the least desire for the existence of weed in his farm and despite the herbicides he uses to destroy them and his [effort to] burn down the farm after the harvest in order to have the weed seeds destroyed, yet, in the next harvest and prior to the crops' growth, we again observe that the weeds have grown. This conveys the message that the farmer has neglected maintaining his farm. As a result of this apparently trivial and venial negligence, the farmer has not gained the favorable yield from his efforts.

The human mind is exactly like a farm which has the possibility both for the growth of flowers or other invaluable products and for poisonous weeds. The farm of our mind is also ruled by the *weed law*. This law evidently shows that any kind of carelessness is equal to losing the product of human's thoughts and them being replaced with weeds.

Experience proves that incorrect thoughts and futile and discourteous teachings which are inconsistent with culture, penetrate into our minds more rapidly than useful and healthy thoughts and teachings, and are even more lasting. For instance, if through similar techniques we teach two groups of students; a [noble] poem by a [well-known] mystic to one group and a poisonous and vulgar poem to the second group, and ask them both to memorize their poems, the second group will succeed in memorizing it faster. In the society we also observe that the poems, speeches, films, stories and inappropriate and poisonous observations leave more impact and are imprinted on the mind much faster than poems, speeches, movies, stories and observations that are insightful.

We sometimes face the same problem in training a child, as they often learn indecent, impolite and meaningless words well by hearing, and we see that this learning happens faster than learning beautiful and meaningful words.

The farm of the human mind is the best ground for the growth of weeds. The danger of weed is that it destroys the main product. The destruction sometimes causes mental deviation and at times it leads to nonsensical and idle talk that is out of the individual's control. Thus, not only should we keep a watchful eye on the farm of our minds, we should also not open our mouth to satire and useless phrases and sentences. We should speak tactfully and keep in mind that *'what is inside the jar leaks outside.'*[10]

The danger of weeds is much more serious in the spiritual world. Generally, in mysticism 'weed' refers to the incorrect worldviews which can damage the correct ones, and deviate the individual from the path of Kamal. This can happen as a result of ignorance or carelessness. If the person does not have the correct criterion for distinguishing between negative and positive awareness and is not able to separate and put aside negative awareness, these [negative] awareness will act as weeds, and they will destroy the consequences of the positive awareness. Incorrect interpretation of the positive awareness is likewise dangerous. Thus, on the path of mysticism, constant vigilance of the mind's farm becomes more essential. For this reason, we should pay heed to the following points;

(1) It is not allowed to carelessly analyze or use the received positive awareness.

(2) At each stage of the [spiritual] path, we must reevaluate our inner transformations to identify and resolve our capacity, worldviews and personality deficiencies.

(3) We cannot neglect Satan's tricks which will act subtly.

15. Balance Law

Even though the universe is constantly going through changes,

---

10- This is a Persian saying that means whatever you keep inside a jar penetrates outside and shows itself. Thus, people's words and actions are the manifestations of their thoughts.

owing to the defined relations between its constituents, each part is momentarily balanced. Every constituent has its own role in creating this balance and the role of no particle can be denied. However, in general there are three types of balances (figure 1);

- The negative static balance
- The neutral static balance
- The positive static balance

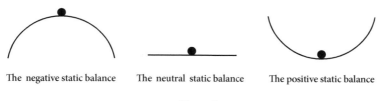

The negative static balance   The neutral static balance   The positive static balance

Figure 1

In the state of *negative static*, when an object goes out of balance [from its original state] it no longer returns to the previous balance. In the state of *neutral static*, when an object moves in a certain direction, it keeps on moving in the same direction, and then regains balance in its new state depending on the direction to which the stimulant factor has redirected it. In the state of *positive static* when an object gets off balance it definitely returns to its balance in the previous state.

There is no absolute balance in objects, and everything is subject to instability and lack of balance. Dynamic balancing also consists of three negative, neutral, and positive states. In any design, the various types of balances are taken into consideration. The best design for any moving object is for the object to be capable of automatically restoring balance. For instance, an airplane is exposed to factors that disrupt its balance, and therefore, it should be designed to automatically return to balance.

On the subject of the human transcendence, the individual's liability to err should also be considered. Accordingly, committing a mistake is not regarded as the person's ultimate downfall. If the person falls into a divergence of no return after making a mistake, they must have been in the state of *negative static*. And, if the person's extreme unawareness persuades them to follow any path without further thinking, they are in the state of *neutral static* balance. However, the best state is the *positive static* balance. In this state, the individual can quite possibly commit a mistake any moment, but after each stray off the axis of stability (each likely stumble) they easily regain their balance (return to their main Kamal-seeking path). Hence, no factor disturbs the individual's overall balance.

In order to reach this type of balance we should first accept our fallibility, and then, in case of committing mistakes, we should return to our main path (desirable balance) and ignore the satanic deceptions that disappoint us from returning to the state of balance. The important point is that the amplitude of mistakes can be narrowed, which promises more stability. (Figure 2)

Figure 2: The process of increased positive static balance

Neglecting the principles relating to the *balance law* leads to our wrong judgments, hopelessness, disappointment, and aberration. Similar to other worldview weaknesses regarding the laws of the universe, this too eventually creates illnesses that are a result of conflicts.